REVELS STUDENT EDITIONS

THE CHANGELING
Thomas Middleton and
William Rowley

MANCHESTER

REVELS STUDENT EDITIONS

Based on the highly respected Revels Plays, which provide a wide range of scholarly critical editions of plays by Shakespeare's contemporaries, the Revels Student Editions offer readable and competitively priced introductions, text and commentary designed to distil the erudition and insights of the Revels Plays, while focusing on matters of clarity and interpretation.

GENERAL EDITOR   David Bevington

REVELS STUDENT EDITIONS

THE CHANGELING
Thomas Middleton and William Rowley

edited by N. W. Bawcutt

based on The Revels Plays edition
edited by N. W. Bawcutt
published by Methuen & Co., 1958
and by Manchester University Press, 1975

MANCHESTER
UNIVERSITY PRESS

Manchester and New York

Distributed exclusively in the USA by
St. Martin's Press

Introduction, critical apparatus, etc.
© N. W. Bawcutt 1998

The right of N. W. Bawcutt to be identified as the editor of this
work has been asserted by him in accordance with the Copyright,
Designs and Patents Act 1988.

Published by Manchester University Press
Oxford Road, Manchester M13 9NR, UK
and Room 400, 175 Fifth Avenue, New York, NY 10010, USA

Distributed exclusively in the USA by
St. Martin's Press, Inc.,
175 Fifth Avenue, New York,
NY 10010, USA

Distributed exclusively in Canada by
UBC Press, University of British Columbia,
6344 Memorial Road,
Vancouver, BC, Canada V6T 1Z2

British Library Cataloguing-in-Publication Data
A catalogue record for this book is available from the British Library

Library of Congress Cataloging-in-Publication Data
Middleton, Thomas, d. 1627.
The changeling / Thomas Middleton and William Rowley: edited by
N. W. Bawcutt.
p. cm.—(Revels student editions)
Includes bibliographical references (pp. 27–8)
ISBN 0-7190-4481-2
I. Rowley, William. 1585?–1626 II. Bawcutt,
N. W. III. Title. IV. Series.
PR2714.C5 1998
822'.3—dc21   97-47409

ISBN 0 7190 4481 2 *paperback*

First published 1998
05 04 03 02 01 00   10 9 8 7 6 5 4 3 2

Typeset
by Best-set Typesetter Ltd., Hong Kong
Printed in Great Britain
by Clays Ltd, St Ives Plc

Introduction

By the time they came to collaborate on *The Changeling*, early in 1622, Middleton and Rowley were experienced and well-established dramatists. Thomas Middleton, the more famous of the two, was born in London in 1580 and died there in 1627. His father died in January 1586, and his mother re-married in November of the same year; unfortunately the stepfather was a dubious character whose escapades embroiled the family in quarrels and lawsuits. Middleton was educated at Queen's College, Oxford, where he subscribed on entry to the college on 7 April 1598, but there were financial problems and he seems to have left Oxford without taking a degree by the beginning of 1601. He began his career as an author in the last years of the sixteenth century, writing various poems and satirical pamphlets, and collaborating in a number of plays for Henslowe's company, all now lost, with such dramatists as Munday, Dekker, and Webster.

Middleton's activities as a dramatist cover the first quarter of the seventeenth century. His early plays, often written for boys' companies, were mostly satirical city comedies of sexual and financial intrigue, though he also wrote tragedy, especially if, as many scholars now believe, he was the author of *The Revenger's Tragedy*, published in 1607. Later he turned more to tragicomedy and tragedy; the most famous of his independently written tragedies, *Women Beware Women*, is set in Renaissance Florence but contains much to remind the audience of contemporary London. *A Game at Chess*, an audacious satire in which English and Spanish political relations are presented in terms of a chess game, caused a minor sensation when it was performed in 1624. He also had close ties with the City of London, and between 1613 and 1626 wrote many of the pageants that were given yearly by one or other of the great Livery Companies to welcome the new Lord Mayor.

William Rowley's date of birth and family background are not known, and nearly all the information we have about him derives from his connections with the stage. The earliest record of Rowley

1

as an actor, dated 1609, links him with the company patronised by Prince Charles, later Charles I; Rowley's name appears on documents related to the company, and he was evidently a leading member, several times receiving payment for court performances by the company. For the last two or three years of his life (he died in February 1626) he was a member of the King's company. He was also a prolific dramatist, employing a wide variety of themes and genres, and he frequently wrote in collaboration with other drama- tists. Partly because of this a precise and accurate canon of his plays has never been established, and only a few of the plays with which he was connected are available in good modern editions.

COLLABORATION

The collaboration of Middleton and Rowley extended over several years, and the two men may have been friends as well as collabora- tors: it has, for example, been plausibly suggested that Middleton introduced the character of the Fat Bishop into *A Game at Chess* partly in order to provide a good role for Rowley, who was appar- ently very corpulent. He also played the part of Plumporridge in Middleton's *The Inner Temple Masque*, performed early in 1619. Rowley specialised in comic roles, and performed the part of Jacques, 'a simple clownish gentleman', in his own play, *All's Lost by Lust* (?1619–20). It is tempting to speculate, though there is nothing to prove it, that he played Lollio in *The Changeling*. The two men collaborated as dramatists several times: in *A Fair Quarrel*, published 1617, *The World Tossed at Tennis*, published 1620, and perhaps *The Spanish Gipsy*, licensed for performance on 9 July 1623 but not published until 1653.[1]

The distribution of scenes in *The Changeling* between Middleton and Rowley was first established by late nineteenth-century scholars. Rowley was responsible for the opening and closing scenes of the play and for the sub-plot set in Alibius's madhouse; Middleton wrote all the intervening scenes of the main plot. This gives the following division:

I.i, I.ii	Rowley
II.i, II.ii	Middleton
III.i, III.ii	Middleton
III.iii	Rowley
III.iv	Middleton

IV.i, IV.ii	Middleton
IV.iii	Rowley
V.i, V.ii	Middleton
V.iii	Rowley

In recent years the tests used to discriminate authorship have become increasingly sophisticated, and tend now to rely on minute features of verbal and grammatical usage rather than, as in the past, on material such as an individual dramatist's use of large-scale metaphors. But to a striking degree whatever tests are used support and confirm each other. The only modification recently made to the division given above is that the first sixteen lines of IV.ii are now thought to be by Rowley.

It is clear that the collaboration between Middleton and Rowley in *The Changeling* was unusually close and intimate. There are none of the confusions and inconsistencies that sometimes result from multiple authorship, and (to put the matter more positively) there is a striking continuity between main plot scenes by Rowley and those by Middleton. All scholars would agree that Middleton was the more sophisticated and accomplished dramatist of the two, but this does not mean that we should treat Rowley as the junior partner. If the division given above is accurate, Rowley wrote slightly more than half the play, and was responsible for such brilliant touches as De Flores' meditation on Beatrice's glove at the end of the opening scene, and Beatrice's speech at V.iii.149–61, possibly the most famous lines in the play. Furthermore, neither Middleton nor Rowley independently wrote work quite as good as their achievements in *The Changeling*; in this particular case collaboration had the effect of inspiring them to new heights.

THE PLAY

The basic story of the main plot was taken from John Reynolds's *The Triumphs of God's Revenge against Murder*, first published in 1621. Reynolds's book is a collection of stories all following the same pattern: greed and sexual desire lead to murder, which may be concealed for some time but is always revealed in the end and punished with death. The source, however, has none of the power and energy of the play. Reynolds's De Flores, for example, is a nonentity, a handsome young man who willingly murders Alonzo but is satisfied with kisses as his reward. He does not become

Beatrice's lover until three months after her marriage, when Alsemero suddenly and unreasonably becomes jealous of his wife. As this shows, the dramatists speed up events which in the source stretch over several months: Acts I to III of the play cover two days, there is then a gap of not more than ten days (see IV.ii.3–14), and Acts IV and V take place on the wedding day and the following day (the marriage lasts for only one day).

Although attempts have been made to link it with numerous earlier plays, *The Changeling* is a fresh and independent work. It does indeed contain some traces of stock dramatic conventions—a ghost and a revenger—but the ghost is a shadowy mute who is easily brushed aside by his murderers, and the revenger is helpless and frustrated, even at one point ignorantly appealing to his brother's murderer for information. There is a high degree of realism and psychological plausibility in the play, and in tone it is closer to domestic tragedies like the anonymous *Arden of Faversham* or Heywood's *A Woman Killed with Kindness* than to lurid court tragedy such as *The Revenger's Tragedy* or Webster's *The White Devil*.

There is violence and bloodshed in the play, but it is never merely gratuitous. When De Flores hacks off Alonzo's ring-finger in III.ii the incident, not found in Reynolds's version of the story, is grotesque and horrible (and is felt as such by the audience), but is made to bear a rich and multiple significance. It exposes the callous ruthlessness of De Flores, happy to mutilate as well as murder his victim. It symbolises how Alonzo's foolish fidelity to Beatrice has led to his destruction: even in death, it seems, he will not part with the ring she gave him as a love token. Finally, Beatrice's shock when De Flores later produces the finger shows her shallowness, her assumption that the role of De Flores is to carry out the sordid task of murder but not to confront her with the reality of it.

The opening scene is worth analysing in some detail, to show how skilfully Rowley laid the groundwork for future developments in the play. The scene begins with omens which have a dubious significance. Alsemero hesitates to commit himself to his sudden and unexpected love for Beatrice because he met her in church, not an appropriate place to begin a love affair, but he manages to smother his doubt by giving the omen a favourable interpretation. Totally conflicting assertions are made as to whether the signs indicate that this is a propitious day to travel to Malta. It is the 'critical day' (line 49) in the fullest sense: decisions made now will be crucially significant. Phrases such as 'hidden malady' (24) and 'this smoke will bring forth fire' (51–2) suggest that there are unpleasant secrets which will sooner or later come to light.

The use of the words 'change' or 'changed', which occur nineteen times in the play as a whole, helps to reinforce the idea that we are witnessing a vital turning point in the characters' lives. Alsemero is transformed from a hardened soldier and traveller, indifferent to women and restlessly anxious to move on to his next destination, into an ardent lover, a change which Jasperino observes with amazement. Yet he does not seem entirely happy in his new role, although Diaphanta's later comment at V.i.78 shows that he does not lack sexual drive. Beatrice too shows a 'giddy turning' (I.i.158). Later in the play she presents herself as the victimised girl being forced into marriage by an overbearing father and a hated but persistent suitor. Yet at III.iv.143 De Flores accuses her of having changed from her 'first love' Alonzo to her second, Alsemero, and phrases like 'Sure, mine eyes were mistaken; / This was the man was meant me' (I.i.85–6) suggest that she became engaged to Alonzo without excessive reluctance, and realised her error only a few days later, on encountering Alsemero, to whom she abruptly transferred her affection.

Alsemero and Beatrice are aware of the importance of making correct decisions, based on clear-sighted observation. Somewhat ironically, the fullest statement of this theme is by Beatrice herself:

> Our eyes are sentinels unto our judgements,
> And should give certain judgement what they see;
> But they are rash sometimes and tell us wonders
> Of common things, which when our judgements find,
> They can then check the eyes and call them blind.   (I.i.73–7)

As moral aphorisms these are fairly banal, with none of the quirky brilliance of writers like Blake or Nietzsche or D. H. Lawrence. Even so, they contain an essential truth: Beatrice comes to disaster through her repeated failures to make accurate assessments of other people. At the same time, and in a rather contradictory way, Beatrice and Alsemero are conscious of the irrationality of much human behaviour, the way in which our likes and dislikes have no reasonable justification (I.i.110–29). De Flores can see no cause for Beatrice's dislike of him but a 'peevish will' (108), yet at the end of the scene he resolves to go on obtruding himself into her presence, even if it produces no benefit: 'Though I get nothing else, I'll have my will' (239). Vermandero is determined to have his will in getting

Alonzo as a son-in-law; Beatrice is equally determined to have her own will in the matter.

Finally, there are some splendid dramatic ironies in the opening scene, though their full power will be apparent only when we return to them with a full knowledge of the play. Vermandero must be cautious about admitting strangers to his castle because 'within are secrets' (168), presumably of a military nature. Later he discovers with horror that there are all kinds of secrets within his castle that have been concealed from him (V.iii.147–8). Beatrice protests at being rushed into marriage because she wishes to surrender her virginity in a dignified and ceremonious way. Obviously she cannot know at this point of the circumstances, at the end of Act III, in which she will lose her virginity. Alsemero is reluctant to enter Vermandero's castle 'When he discharges murderers at the gate' (I.i.225). 'Murderers' are small cannon, and Alsemero is using a variant of the language of courtly love: the news that his beloved is to marry someone else has struck him dead. It turns out, of course, that there will be murderers in the castle of a very different kind.

From Act II onwards, as far as Act V, scene ii, Middleton was responsible for the main plot. Acts II and III show the explosive transformation of the relationship between Beatrice and De Flores, and contain some of the most subtle and penetrating writing for the stage to be found in the whole of English drama. For a second time Beatrice violently abuses De Flores, but then suddenly realises that she could make use of him, and what appears to be a kind of reconciliation takes place. But this is based on mutual misunderstandings which are brutally exposed when De Flores returns to claim his reward for having killed Alonzo. All this is revealed to the audience with remarkable intimacy and fullness of detail, partly achieved through the use of soliloquies and asides. In other dramatists these can be no more than conventional and obtrusive devices, but here they are smoothly integrated into the flow of the play.

Beatrice and De Flores are not deeply complex characters, but they are brought to life for us with remarkable power. De Flores, it is clear, lives for only one thing, his unwavering obsession with Beatrice which leads him to push himself continually into her company, even though he receives nothing but abuse for doing so. We might even be reminded of that repulsive modern phenomenon, the 'stalker' who becomes fixated on a particular person and will not leave her or him alone, though the modern stalker is usually a stranger to the victim, whereas De Flores is a family servant and it is part of his duties to carry messages to Beatrice. The beginning of Act II shows a typical example. De Flores has been ordered to let Beatrice know of the arrival of Alonzo, and spins out his announcement in elaborately formal language so as to prolong his time in her presence, to the mounting exasperation of Beatrice.

It is sometimes argued that De Flores understands Beatrice in a way that the other characters do not. He could be said to spy on her, and knows what she has been doing better than anyone else, but his interpretation of her psychology is not strikingly perceptive. For him violent sexual passion is 'beyond all reason' (II.i.84), and he knows that beautiful women have sometimes 'doted' on faces much uglier than his own (he elaborates on the repulsive details with relish, II.i.40–5). He will therefore doggedly persist in his pursuit of Beatrice, in the hope that one day her resistance will suddenly collapse, though it is surely very unlikely that Beatrice would have become his mistress merely through the passage of time. After watching her secret meeting with Alsemero De Flores assumes, quite wrongly, that she intends to marry Alonzo but take Alsemero as a lover. He is pleased, because to his cynical mind a married woman who takes one lover will automatically take hundreds more. At this point he does not mind how degraded she becomes because it will increase his chances of becoming one of her lovers.

If De Flores sometimes makes misjudgements, he has an underlying shrewdness and toughness that enable him to recover from them. The same is hardly true for Beatrice. She is impressed by Jasperino's efficient conduct as a go-between for Alsemero; this shows Alsemero's wisdom in choosing him as friend, and enables her to congratulate herself on her own wisdom in choosing Alsemero as her lover. (There may be a touch of dramatic irony here, since it is Jasperino's loyalty as a friend that makes Alsemero become suspicious of her later in the play.) She enunciates a general rule:

> For 'tis a principle, he that can choose
> That bosom well, who of his thoughts partakes,
> Proves most discreet in every choice he makes.   (II.i.10–12)

Then, drawing on the 'eyes' and 'judgement' theme established in the opening scene, she praises her own clear-sightedness: 'Methinks I love now with the eyes of judgement, / And see the way to merit, clearly see it' (II.i.13–14). But the rest of the play shows that when forced to choose someone to trust and rely on—first De Flores, then

Diaphanta, and finally Alsemero himself—she goes disastrously wrong.

There is a revealing touch at II.i.92–3: 'The next good mood I find my father in, / I'll get him quite discarded. . . .' Vermandero is not simply the tyrannical patriarch; he is also the affectionate father who can be manipulated by his daughter if she chooses her time skilfully. Beatrice has something in her of the spoilt child, who sees other people existing only to further her wishes, and is shocked and indignant when they turn out to have their own independent purposes. But her treatment of Vermandero, it must be said, is reasonably successful. By the beginning of Act III, scene iv, she has secured 'the liberty of the house' (12) for Alsemero, presumably implying that he can visit the castle whenever he likes. This gives her another chance to congratulate herself ('So wisdom by degrees works out her freedom', III.iv.13), and she is serenely confident that her father will eventually be persuaded to accept Alsemero as a son-in-law.

The two finest scenes in the play are II.ii, in which Beatrice engages De Flores to murder Alonzo, and III.iv, in which he returns to claim his reward. II.ii opens with the secret rendezvous of Beatrice and Alsemero, and ironically it is Alsemero's attitude which prompts Beatrice's behaviour a little later. She has complained of a double problem, in that pressure is being put on her both by her fiancé and by her father. Alsemero offers an 'honourable' solution: he will challenge Alonzo de Piracquo immediately, presumably in order to kill him, and this will deal with both problems simultaneously. Beatrice is horrified, but there is a curious one-sidedness in her response. She is not shocked at the idea of killing Alonzo, only at the risk this will pose to Alsemero, who may be punished by the law if he succeeds in the duel, or have to live as a fugitive. She also has an aesthetic or perhaps we should say squeamish response: Alsemero is too handsome a gentleman to become dirtied with 'Blood-guiltiness' (II.ii.40).

Beatrice then experiences a sudden flash of inspiration, a spark which ignites the play. De Flores is the perfect answer to her problems, a repulsively ugly man for whom a sordid and defiling task would be quite appropriate. As we learn at the end of the scene, she also assumes that he will conveniently vanish after being rewarded for carrying out her task:

> I shall rid myself
> Of two inveterate loathings at one time,
> Piracquo, and his dog-face.   (II.ii.144–6)

Though she rebukes herself for having been rude to De Flores, her tone is one of immense self-satisfaction: her solution to the problem is very much better than Alsemero's, and like his will achieve two goals simultaneously. In her delight at having found an ingenious way of escape she becomes increasingly unaware of Alsemero ('Lady, you hear not me', II.ii.48). Though she had ordered him to conceal nothing from her, she makes no attempt to share her thoughts with him, and unceremoniously gets rid of him as soon as she can.

De Flores has been watching the interview, and is aware that interesting developments are taking place that he does not fully understand, though they seem to hint at a developing promiscuity in Beatrice which he finds promising. Both he and Beatrice are nervously excited in their ensuing encounter, and become increasingly tense as they gradually reach an arrangement which will apparently fulfil the deepest wishes for both of them. Obviously this will not be the case, but what needs to be stressed is that the mutual misunderstanding is equally deep on both sides. De Flores is the villain of the play, but does not become the controlling spirit of his partnership with Beatrice until later. The plan to get rid of Alonzo has been devised by Beatrice herself, and she puts herself in De Flores' power by summoning him to collaborate without adequately considering the consequences.

With conscious hypocrisy Beatrice begins her pretence of an altered attitude towards De Flores. In the past she had called him 'Thou standing toad-pool', 'Slave', and 'Thou thing most loathed' (II.i.58, 68, 72). (We should remember that in Elizabethan English the second person singular pronouns 'thou' and 'thee' could be used to indicate superiority and contempt.) Now, for the first time in the play, she simply addresses him by name, a significant shift which he recognises with delight:

> Ha, I shall run mad with joy;
> She called me fairly by my name De Flores,
> And neither 'rogue' nor 'rascal'!   (II.ii.70–2)

She also uses 'Sir' and the neutral pronoun 'you'. Of course, she goes much further than this. De Flores now looks 'amorously' (75) (both lovely and lovable), and she terms him 'my De Flores' (98), as though he is now an accepted lover. This is playing with fire, and triggers in De Flores an intensity of response which Beatrice wrongly assumes to derive from poverty and financial greed.

De Flores eagerly agrees to carry out her wishes, but misinterprets her manoeuvring in a way which will prove disastrous to her. He has a sturdy common sense that makes him sceptical when she asserts that his looks have improved:

> Not I;
> 'Tis the same physnomy, to a hair and pimple,
> Which she called scurvy scarce an hour ago.   (II.ii.75–7)

Yet when she persists he can only assume that the long-awaited change of feeling has at last come about, and that in her voracious sexual appetite Beatrice now sees him as a source of sexual pleasure despite his ugliness:

> Methinks I feel her in mine arms already,
> Her wanton fingers combing out this beard,
> And, being pleased, praising this bad face.   (II.ii.147–9)

Underneath this is a hint of contempt towards her ('Some women are odd feeders', 153). He may be obsessed by her, and regard possession of her as the supreme value of his life, to the achieving of which anything else will gladly be sacrificed, but his attitude towards her shows no trace of idealism, rather the reverse.

In III.i and III.ii the murder is briskly and efficiently carried out, and in III.iv De Flores returns to claim his reward. Ironically, Beatrice weeps for joy at the news of Alsemero's death, but is startled and horrified when De Flores produces the severed finger of Alonzo as proof that he has accomplished his task. For the first time De Flores performs a function that he is to carry out several times in the remainder of the scene, that of disabusing Beatrice, stripping away her false assumptions and misunderstandings. To cut off a finger is hardly worse than 'killing the whole man', and is in any case a triviality: 'A greedy hand thrust in a dish at court / In a mistake hath had as much as this' (III.iv.31–2). In a characteristically reductive image De Flores compares his mutilation of Alonzo's corpse to the way in which greedy hangers-on at court hack with their knives at a joint of meat, and in so doing risk the loss of a finger.

Beatrice shows a slight touch of wistfulness: ''Tis the first token my father made me send him' (33), but De Flores is more down-to-earth ('dead men have no use of jewels', 36). Once again Alonzo's stubbornness is symbolically registered: 'He was as loath to part with't, for it stuck / As if the flesh and it were both one substance' (37–8). (Compare III.ii.23–4.) Beatrice offers the ring to De Flores, and is surprised when he accepts it grudgingly: 'Why, thou mistak'st, De Flores, 'tis not given / In state of recompense' (49–50). The language is simple, but brilliantly conveys an ambiguity: the two participants have very different ideas of what form the further recompense will take. There is a similar ambiguity with 'misery' (see the commentary on III.iv.58); at each point De Flores attaches a grimmer and more powerful meaning to the term than Beatrice does.

At lines 61–2 Beatrice makes what she regards as a final offer of three thousand florins, making it unmistakably clear that her notion of payment is solely financial. De Flores is outraged, and there is even a hint that he is angered by the size of the sum, presumably larger than he had expected:

> I could ha' hired
> A journeyman in murder at this rate,
> And mine own conscience might have slept at ease ...   (68–70)

At this point De Flores seems to share Beatrice's assumption that moral guilt can be projected on to someone else by paying that person to perform an evil deed, but he does not carry this through into the later part of the scene. Beatrice's attempts to pay him more and to get him to flee are brushed aside, but her reluctance to understand what he really wants forces him into a totally explicit statement:

> ... were I not resolved in my belief
> That thy virginity were perfect in thee,
> I should but take my recompense with grudging,
> As if I had but half my hopes I agreed for.   (116–19)

Earlier he had been prepared to share her with others, but now he will be the man to take her virginity, a factor which doubles his pleasure.

Beatrice's reply is magnificent:

> Why, 'tis impossible thou canst be so wicked,
> Or shelter such a cunning cruelty,
> To make his death the murderer of my honour!
> Thy language is so bold and vicious,
> I cannot see which way I can forgive it
> With any modesty.   (120–5)

She is still the aristocratic young lady who instinctively shelters behind the language of morality and gentility. De Flores ruthlessly strips away her defences one by one: as a 'woman dipped in blood' (126), a murderess, she cannot use her social position as a barrier against him. In a splendid phrase, she is 'the deed's creature' (137) and her partner now will be De Flores. Her last desperate attempt to buy him off with the whole of her fortune is met with lines 'of which Shakespeare or Sophocles might have been proud':[2] 'Can you weep fate from its determined purpose? / So soon may you weep me' (162–3). He raises and embraces the shuddering girl, carrying her off with words that might contain a hint of tenderness: ' 'Las, how the turtle pants! Thou'lt love anon / What thou so fear'st and faint'st to venture on' (170–1). This is close to a couplet in Ben Jonson's marriage masque *Hymenaei*, lines 453–4: 'Shrink not, soft virgin, you will love / Anon, what you so fear to prove'. But in De Flores' mouth the words have a sinister resonance; this is not the nervousness any girl might feel before what she hopes will prove a loving and happy marriage. Beatrice will come to love and depend on a man she previously feared and hated.

MIDDLETON'S STYLE

Middleton's verse style is strikingly appropriate to the tone of the play. Its qualities can be defined partly in terms of negatives: there are no obvious displays of rhetoric, no 'purple passages' which can be easily detached to stand on their own. Unlike Webster, for example, he avoids crowding his text with elaborate sententiae, proverbs, moral fables, and other decorative features. This does not, of course, mean that Middleton never uses stylistic devices, but he has the gift of blending them smoothly and unobtrusively into the characters' meditations and conversations. At times the lines read like colloquial utterance which has naturally and spontaneously taken on the rhythm of blank verse: 'A woman dipped in blood, and talk of modesty?' (III.iv.126). The audience is invited, not to pause and admire the verse for its own sake, but to register its meaning and significance in a rapidly evolving context.

Middleton very rarely employs unusual words or coinages; though no studies have been made of his dramatic vocabulary, it is probably only a fraction of Shakespeare's. But he has the gift of charging this ordinary language with remarkable intensity. This can apply to words that might normally seem a little bland. For example, he frequently uses the word 'peace' in the sense 'peace of mind', which possibly suggests a relaxed state of contentment. But when the word is used by De Flores after Beatrice's resistance has collapsed ('Thy peace is wrought for ever in this yielding', III.iv.169) or by Tomazo as he prepares to kill what he thinks are the murderers of his brother ('you have brought a peace / The riches of five kingdoms could not purchase', V.ii.83–4), it takes on a grim resonance. Paradoxically, De Flores uses the words 'sweet' and 'sweets' more frequently than any other character, but in his mouth they are applied to intense sexual pleasure in a way that deprives them of any hint of sentimentality.

Other ways in which Middleton achieves intensity include the use of a savagely powerful irony. Shortly before killing Alonzo, De Flores speaks like a tour-guide promising an unexpected wonder: 'All this is nothing; you shall see anon / A place you little dream on' (III.ii.1–2). In Act V Beatrice encounters Diaphanta after she has stayed too long in Alsemero's bed, and orders her to go to her room:

Beatrice.   Hie quickly to your chamber;
  Your reward follows you.
Diaphanta.   I never made
  So sweet a bargain.   (V.i.79–81)

The language is commonplace, even banal, but is brought to life by the brutal hypocrisy of Beatrice and the naive unawareness of Diaphanta. Later in the scene Alsemero orders Beatrice not to mourn any longer for Diaphanta: 'I charge you, by the last embrace I gave you / In bed before this raised us', to which she replies: 'Now you tie me; / Were it my sister, now she gets no more' (110–12). The scene culminates in Beatrice's request that De Flores be rewarded for his care in attending to the fire he started, a device that arouses his cynical admiration (V.i.125–7).

At times the irony shades off into a pun, as when De Flores says of the sconce in which he intends to bury Alonzo, 'There you may dwell awhile' (see the commentary on III.ii.14). Alonzo replies 'I am upon't', meaning 'Now I see it'; De Flores picks up his phrase ('And so am I'), but obviously implies something like 'I am hitting my target'. Some words have a sexual double meaning: 'blood' can mean lust or the bodily fluid; 'service' can refer to assistance and helpfulness or to copulation; 'act' and 'deed' can be the sexual act or the murder of Alonzo. This aspect of the play has been brilliantly analysed by Christopher Ricks,[3] who is careful, however, to stress that the words do not necessarily have a double meaning at every use, and that the characters themselves are not always employing them as a deliberate and conscious play on words.

Middleton's images are rarely exotic. Often the two elements of the comparison are so close together that we lose sight of them as similes or metaphors:

> As children cry themselves asleep, I ha' seen
> Women have chid themselves abed to men.   (II.i.87–8)

> These women are the ladies' cabinets;
> Things of most precious trust are locked into 'em.   (II.ii.6–7)

A simile at II.i.15: 'A true deserver like a diamond sparkles . . .' turns into reality at III.ii.20–1: 'Ha! What's that / Threw sparkles in my eye? Oh, 'tis a diamond . . .' suggesting that whatever his faults may be Alonzo is a 'true deserver' who suffers a horribly unjust fate. Middleton repeatedly applies images of eating and drinking to an intense desire which may be for killing (compare the use of 'thirst' at II.ii.133 and V.ii.85), or for sexuality ('My thoughts are at a banquet for the deed', III.iv.18), or, more rarely, for money ('Gold tastes like angels' food', II.ii.126). It is the opposite of the imagery found in Metaphysical poetry, which expands outward into unexpected areas; in Middleton strange, even perverted, states of mind are, as it were, domesticated, made more real and substantial by being embedded in normal human experience.

THE SUB-PLOT

The sub-plot, written by Rowley, is set in a madhouse. This feature is not unique: other contemporary plays, such as Dekker and Webster's *Northward Ho* and Fletcher's *The Pilgrim*, contain madhouse scenes. All of them are modelled to some extent on a real asylum of the period, Bethlehem Hospital in Bishopsgate, London, whose name was shortened to 'Bedlam', though they are not to be taken as portrayals of the historical institution. Alibius runs a private madhouse, which is also his home (I.i.34), and he regards it as a commercial business ('My trade, my living 'tis, I thrive by it', I.ii.51). This approach extends to the treatment of his patients, who can be seen by the public as a spectacle, as was the case with Bethlehem Hospital (we are told of 'daily visitants' at I.ii.53, though none is shown on stage). He also uses his patients to provide crude entertainment at a wedding ceremony, a new venture he seems anxious to develop. His young wife Isabella is critical of his attitude: 'You've a fine trade on't; / Madmen and fools are a staple commodity' (III.iii.277–8). But he pleads economic necessity ('Oh, wife, we must eat, wear clothes, and live', 279). Discipline is maintained with a whip, and there are hints that the patients may not be well fed (I.ii.197–211).

It is unlikely, however, that contemporary audiences would have been shocked by Alibius's behaviour. Madness was regarded at the time with a robust lack of sympathy which we should now consider to be outright brutality. Isabella initially reacts to Franciscus with some sensitivity: 'Alack, alack, 'tis too full of pity / To be laughed at . . .' (III.iii.45–6). This shows an admirable humaneness, but also a revealing assumption that most people will find him ludicrous. It does seem, however, that Rowley is using folly and madness for comic purposes, not to create horror. Particularly in the opening scene of the sub-plot, there is a stream of jokes about fools and knaves, with satire on the stupidity of officials such as constables and justices (the latter picked up again by Diaphanta at IV.i.127), and the dishonesty of lawyers, tailors, and pluralist clergymen. The mockery is all-embracing: when Isabella complains of being confined to the company of fools and madmen, Lollio replies, 'Very well; and where will you find any other, if you should go abroad?' (III.iii.16–17).

The central target for mockery is the foolish behaviour of lovers. We are shown Antonio the fool and Franciscus the madman, but it soon becomes clear that they are would-be lovers of Isabella in disguise, and the real patients make only fleeting appearances. The sub-plot is a comedy of love intrigue, but the intrigues are doomed to collapse into bathetic failure. Usually in Jacobean comedy a foolish old husband with a pretty young wife will be cuckolded sooner or later. Here the pattern is inverted, and a loyal wife outwits the men who wish to seduce her. Isabella is like Beatrice in having three lovers ardently pursuing her; unlike Beatrice she has an innate honesty and strength of mind that enable her to escape disaster. By the end of the play the husband recognises his error and promises to treat her with more respect in future.

In several ways the sub-plot echoes and parallels the main plot. There are similarities of plot, but they are used to very different effect. After Lollio has overheard Antonio revealing his love to Isabella in III.iii he tries to blackmail her in the same way that De

Flores coerces Beatrice in the next scene. But Isabella counters this by threatening to have Antonio treat Lollio in the way De Flores treated Alonzo:

> Be silent, mute,
> Mute as a statue, or his injunction
> For me enjoying shall be to cut thy throat.   (III.iii.242–4)

The two threats have the effect of cancelling themselves out, so that in the end nothing actually happens. Later Antonio and Franciscus are each told separately by Lollio that he can earn Isabella's love by ridding her of the unwelcome attentions of his rival (IV.iii.149–59 and 190–205), rather as De Flores gets rid of Alonzo. It is sometimes assumed that they are supposed to kill each other, but all that is involved is a thumping ('Bang but his fool's coat well-favouredly, and 'tis well', IV.iii.201–2). The lovers have made fools of themselves in a variety of senses (see the commentary on III.iii.148).

The title of the play, *The Changeling* (i.e. the fool or idiot), refers in the first place, as the Dramatis Personae makes clear, to Antonio, a figure in the sub-plot. Early audiences seem to have found him irresistibly funny, and comic actors such as William Robbins, Timothy Reade, and Thomas Sheppey were celebrated for their performances as 'the changeling'. (See also the commentary on I.ii.82.1.) Clearly the play owed its title and a good deal of its popularity to the sub-plot. This may seem strange to modern taste, but we should compare another tragedy by Middleton now usually called *Hengist, King of Kent*. In the middle seventeenth century this was normally known as *The Mayor of Quinborough*, and was published under this title in 1661, though the comic scenes set in Quinborough, or Queenborough, in Kent occupy only a small part of the play.

Some critics have noticed what they regard as deficiencies in the sub-plot, of a kind that might point to gaps or omissions in the text of the play. No arrangements are made for the introduction of Antonio and Franciscus into the madhouse; the wedding entertainment is not performed before its intended audience; and the quarrel between Antonio and Franciscus is not resolved. All these points can be answered. As Antonio and Franciscus are rivals, two separate scenes would be needed to explain their intention; this would be clumsy, and in any case there is no reason why the audience should not discover the truth about them in the same way as Isabella does.

A rehearsal of the wedding entertainment is given at the end of Act IV, and a second performance is hardly necessary. (It is made clear at III.iii.260 and IV.iii.55–6 that it will not be performed on the wedding night itself, and the play ends on the day after the wedding.) The quarrel between Antonio and Franciscus will merely end in a scuffle, as we have seen, and it is not essential that this should be shown on stage.

ACTS IV AND V

No later scene has the power and brilliance of III.iv, but this does not mean that the end of the play is an anti-climax. Beatrice's shuddering surrender to De Flores at the end of Act III is only one of the consequences of her thoughtless plotting, and the audience needs to see her as 'the deed's creature' (III.iv.137) in a variety of ways. At the beginning of Act II she had praised Alsemero's wisdom and judgement, qualities which justified her choice of him as a lover; now, in IV.i, his abilities make him a dangerous opponent who will discover her loss of virginity and condemn her for it:

> One that's ennobled both in blood and mind,
> So clear in understanding (that's my plague now),
> Before whose judgement will my fault appear
> Like malefactors' crimes before tribunals . . .   (IV.i.5–8)

She makes no attempt to question the assumption that a young woman of high social status must be a virgin when she marries, and even accepts that it would be an act of 'justice' (IV.i.14) for Alsemero to strangle her when he discovers the truth.

Much of IV.i and IV.ii is taken up with the virginity test undergone by Diaphanta and Beatrice. Modern audiences are likely to find it merely ludicrous, and the play itself describes the test as a 'merry sleight' (IV.i.45) and 'the strangest trick to know a maid by' (IV.ii.142). It is plausible that Alsemero should be an amateur physician (Beatrice offers to make a lotion to cure De Flores' skin disease at II.ii.83–4). But it does seem strange that as a confirmed bachelor before the play opens he should carry round with him pregnancy and virginity tests. Perhaps we should consider the device not for the light it sheds on Alsemero but for the way in which it shows that Beatrice's initial wrongdoing leads her into a succession of further problems involving plotting and deception. The symptoms of the test—gaping, sneezing, and laughing—are unimpresssive, but Middleton had to think of something immediate and easily actable.

When she sees Diaphanta a 'trick' comes into Beatrice's mind (IV.i.54–5). She repeats her behaviour with De Flores: a sudden inspiration is immediately put into practice, with no attempt to weigh up any possible drawbacks. Diaphanta turns out to be genuinely a virgin, but her eagerness to take Beatrice's place on the wedding night, and a succession of *double entendres*, suggest that she may not prove reliable. She does not, and at the beginning of Act V Beatrice is fuming with self-righteous anger at Diaphanta's untrustworthiness, that she 'serves her own ends' (V.i.2) without considering Beatrice's own needs. But this resentment seems hypocritical from someone who herself 'cannot rule her blood to keep her promise' (V.i.7). Beatrice is horrified when Alsemero calls her a whore at the end of the play (V.iii.31–5), but here she does not hesitate to term Diaphanta a 'whore' (V.i.23) and 'strumpet' (V.i.2 and 64).

Beatrice is now tougher and more brutal: Diaphanta must die, though it is De Flores who devises the method of killing her, and carries it out. (Both of them seem to know instinctively and without discussion that Diaphanta must be disposed of.) Beatrice and De Flores are now fellow conspirators, intimately whispering together, but De Flores is the dominant partner, and Beatrice's attempts to assert herself are decisively snubbed (there is a touch of pathos when, rebuked for trusting Diaphanta, she replies 'I must trust somebody', V.i.15). Clearly the person she now most trusts is De Flores, and she is deeply impressed by his decisive speed and energy, though she still finds him repulsively ugly: 'How heartily he serves me! His face loathes one, / But look upon his care, who would not love him?' (V.i.70–1). He is now 'a man worth loving' and 'A wondrous necessary man' (V.i.76, 91); she is emotionally dependent on him, and his prophecy at the end of Act III has come true.

Rowley was responsible for the final scene, V.iii. Alsemero and Jasperino have witnessed a meeting, not presented on stage, between Beatrice and De Flores in the castle garden, in which they behave as intimate friends, perhaps even kissing (V.iii.52–3). There had been earlier suspicion that Beatrice's proclaimed dislike of De Flores was hypocritical (IV.ii.89–102), and Alsemero is now convinced of her infidelity, though apparently at this point he does not suspect her of any more than adultery. For the third and final time Beatrice makes a misjudgement of character: she confesses to the murder of Alonzo, assuming that Alsemero will see this as proving that she loved him so deeply she was prepared to do anything to secure him as a husband. It will also prove, as she thinks, that De Flores is simply her collaborator in crime and not her lover. Alsemero is horrified; his premonitions at the beginning of the play have been confirmed.

The entry of De Flores allows Alsemero to confront him with Beatrice's confession, though this is done in a grimly ironic and indirect manner that shows Rowley writing like Middleton at his best. Alsemero and De Flores have a verbal fencing match that ends with De Flores revealing precisely what Beatrice most wanted to conceal. He throws the word 'whore' in Alsemero's face (V.iii.107) in a deliberately insulting and provocative way. Even at this late stage, however, Beatrice continues to deny her infidelity. This merely infuriates Alsemero, who sends De Flores in to her and orders the couple to copulate as a rehearsal for the performance they will be giving in hell before an audience of devils. If they do so, the 'horrid sounds' of Beatrice's cries at lines 139–40 could be sexual in origin, but this occurs only twenty-five lines later, and she is carried out wounded immediately afterwards, so it is more likely that she shrieks out as De Flores stabs her. De Flores' comment, 'Nay, I'll along for company' (140), indicates that he intends to kill himself as well and accompany Beatrice in death.

Beatrice makes one more revelation to Alsemero, that he was duped on his wedding night, but it is left to De Flores to add the final touch, that he and Beatrice 'coupled' while waiting for Diaphanta. Beatrice's last speech is an appeal to Alsemero for forgiveness which goes unanswered. Before committing suicide De Flores gloats over the fact that he has not only taken Beatrice's virginity but also been her sole sexual partner, killing her to ensure that no other man can share in the privilege. He has achieved what he regards as his life's ambition, and is quite content to die.

The entry of all the other surviving characters apart from Jasperino and Lollio indicates that the denouement is near at hand. The riddling exchange at lines 121–32, in which Alsemero sarcastically undercuts the eager assertions of Vermandero, has been dismissed as ludicrous by Raymond Pentzell,[4] but in the hands of good actors there is no reason why it should have to be. Vermandero is horrified at the sight of his wounded daughter, but Beatrice keeps him at a distance. In some of the most powerful and chilling lines of the play she sees herself as corrupt and defiling, diseased blood which has been purged from her father and should be thrown away as refuse. She acknowledges the inescapable destiny that linked her to De Flores, but makes no attempt to glamorise the relationship: her early loathing of him should have taught her that his influence would prove totally destructive.

The play concludes with a rather bleak assessment of what has happened. *The Changeling* is a very distinguished play, but it perhaps falls short of the greatest tragedies in that it leaves the audience with no sense of pity or wasted potentiality for the dead characters. There are some humane touches—Tomazo has changed 'from an ignorant wrath / To knowing friendship' (V.iii.202–3)—but Alsemero, who takes on himself the job of spokesperson, exonerates the survivors from any blame and sees the woman he had once loved merely as a practitioner of 'ugly whoredom' (V.iii.198). The characters in the sub-plot ruefully acknowledge their errors, and the scene ends with Alsemero offering Vermandero the duty as a son that was lacking in Beatrice as a daughter, and advising him, perhaps a little too easily, to forget his sorrow.

STAGE HISTORY

The play was licensed for performance by the current Master of the Revels, Sir John Astley, on 7 May 1622; the earliest recorded production was at court on 4 January 1624. It was put on at the Phoenix theatre in Drury Lane, also known as the Cockpit because it was built in 1616 on the site of a former cockpit. It was a private, enclosed theatre intended for a fashionable audience, and proved to be one of the most successful theatres of the early seventeenth century, rivalled only by the Blackfriars theatre, used by the King's company for whom Shakespeare had written. The Phoenix was owned and managed by a former actor named Christopher Beeston, and it is clear that the performing rights of *The Changeling* were vested in Beeston himself rather than in the various acting companies that occupied his theatre. The play was continuously popular down to the closing of the theatres in 1642; it was revived at the Restoration in 1660, and the last recorded performance of the seventeenth century was at the court of Charles II on 30 November 1668.

Until the second half of the twentieth century *The Changeling* dropped from sight on the stage, but repeated productions from 1950 onwards have shown its potentialities in the modern theatre.[5] It was performed, to give selected examples only, in 1961 at the Royal Court Theatre, London, with Mary Ure and Robert Shaw as Beatrice and De Flores, and at the Riverside Studios, London, in

1978, with Emma Piper and Brian Cox. The Royal Shakespeare Company performed the play in 1978, with Diana Quick and Emrys James, and in 1992–93, with Cheryll Campbell and Malcolm Storry. It was shown at the National Theatre in 1988, with Miranda Richardson and George Harris. Some productions reached a mass audience. There were BBC radio broadcasts in November 1950 and June 1960, and there have been three television versions: Granada Television, 4 January 1965, with Kika Markham and Derek Godfrey; BBC TV on 20 January 1974, with Helen Mirren and Stanley Baker; and again on 11 December 1993, with Elizabeth McGovern and Bob Hoskins. Some productions, including all those on television, omitted the sub-plot; others varied in the degree to which they managed to make the two halves of the play cohere.

SOME RECENT APPROACHES

The analysis made so far broadly reflects attitudes to the play during the fifty or so years following the publication of T. S. Eliot's essay. In recent years these attitudes have been challenged in various ways. Some modern critics, for example, have attacked what seem to them to be the moral and social assumptions underlying the play, though they vary in the degree to which they regard the dramatists as complicit in these assumptions, or as exposing and attacking them. The moral world of the play is not easily summarised. There are several explicitly theological allusions: for example, Alsemero opens the play by arguing that marriage can undo the effects of the Fall and restore man to paradise. De Flores is the 'serpent' (I.i.227, V.iii.66), and Beatrice is like Eve, 'that broken rib of mankind' (V.iii.146). Vermandero says of Beatrice's dead mother that 'heaven has married her to joys eternal' (III.iv.5); at the end of the play Alsemero and Tomazo both assert that Beatrice and De Flores are now damned souls who are destined to the tortures of hell (V.iii.114–20 and 190–5).

There is also frequent use of words with a theological flavour— 'heaven', 'creation', 'saint', 'devil', 'devotion', 'reverence', 'holy', and 'blest' (Beatrice, who has most need of blessing, says 'bless me' four times). But language of this kind can be used metaphorically to convey emotions which are obviously secular, as at I.i.31–5 and II.ii.8–12. At times the vocabulary can be employed in ways which are perverse, if not blasphemous, as when De Flores describes himself as being 'up to the chin in heaven' (II.ii.79), or says 'I was blest / To light upon this minute' (II.ii.90–1). When Tomazo thinks he will learn of his brother's murderers, he cannot apologise too strongly for having been discourteous to Vermandero:

> If you bring that calm,
> Name but the manner I shall ask forgiveness in
> For that contemptuous smile upon you.
> I'll perfect it with reverence that belongs
> Unto a sacred altar.   (V.ii.63–7)

(Tomazo's use of 'reverence' here is similar to De Flores' use at II.ii.123.) The context suggests that he kneels as though about to pray, but he takes things so far that Vermandero is embarrassed and rebukes him.

Side by side with the religious vocabulary is a set of words related to the concept of honour—'honour' itself, 'honourable', 'honest', and 'honesty'. This complex of ideas involves an intense concern with reputation, in men for courage and upright behaviour, and in women for chastity, and the loss of honourable reputation is felt as the most shameful and humiliating of experiences. The concern for honour is shown in its simplest and most overt form in Vermandero. He uses 'name' to mean 'distinguished family name', as in his welcome to Alonzo de Piracquo, 'To whose most noble name our love presents / The addition of a son, our son Alonzo' (II.i.98–9). Tactfully Alonzo replies in the same kind of language: 'The treasury of honour cannot bring forth / A title I should more rejoice in, sir' (100–1). For Beatrice, however, her father is forcing her to marry only to enhance his own 'name' (II.i.20–3), and she wishes that the 'name' of Piracquo did not exist (II.ii.18–19). Vermandero sees the death of Beatrice as destroying his own reputation: 'Oh, my name is entered now in that record / Where till this fatal hour 'twas never read' (V.iii.180–1). Alsemero, however, tries to reassure him that he has not been dishonoured.

The code of honour involves physical violence. For Alsemero the simplest solution to the problem of Alonzo is to kill him in a duel: 'The honourablest piece 'bout man, valour. / I'll send a challenge to Piracquo instantly' (II.ii.27–8). Alonzo himself is normally courteous, but he is infuriated by the slightest hint that Beatrice is not impeccably honourable, and narrowly avoids fighting his own brother (II.i.145–53). In IV.ii Tomazo challenges Alsemero, but does not press the matter because it is Alsemero's wedding day; in V.ii he strikes De Flores and nearly fights with him, and ends the scene by rushing out with the clear intention of killing what he thinks are his brother's murderers.

Terms like 'honour' and 'honest' are used with a certain degree of ambiguity. Beatrice refers to 'honour' more frequently than any other character, but by the end of the play she is desperately struggling to preserve what by now is an obvious sham. She thanks De Flores for arranging to murder Diaphanta: 'I'm forced to love thee now, / 'Cause thou provid'st so carefully for my honour' (V.i.47–8). De Flores, however, is not chivalrous and has other priorities: ''Slid, it concerns the safety of us both, / Our pleasure and continuance' (49–50). Immediately before this scene there is mockery of 'honour' in the sub-plot (IV.iii.91–100). 'Honest' has a range of meanings which there is not space to discuss in full; it can, for example, be applied to a sexually respectable woman, as in Alsemero's blunt enquiry at V.iii.20 ('Are you honest?'). Beatrice tests Diaphanta's 'honesty' and is delighted by a positive result: 'Most honest Diaphanta I dare call thee now' (IV.i.119). But Diaphanta's constant use of obscene double meanings, and her behaviour in Alsemero's bed, suggest a rampant sexuality in her for which 'honest' does not seem the appropriate term.

Both the religious code and the 'honour' code may be felt by a modern audience to be brutal and hypocritical, though the play itself does not seem to endorse them uncritically. It should be remembered, however, that the whole play is predicated on rigid and compulsive codes of behaviour, and could not exist without them. A modern Beatrice would have no problem: she would simply tell her fiancé and father that she had changed her mind and was now going to marry someone else, and she would probably assume that her new lover would not be devastated to discover that she was no longer a virgin.

Other aspects of the play's moral scheme might seem to be less open to objection. Earlier critics, from T. S. Eliot onwards, admired the way in which Beatrice was forced to acknowledge the reality of the deed she had instigated so unthinkingly. Although there were differences of opinion as to precisely how innocent or naive she was at the beginning of the play, this painful inculcation of responsibility was felt to be one of the most impressive features of the play, which was not dependent for its effect on obsolete ways of feeling. Some critics were also impressed by the conclusion of the play, the attempt of the surviving characters to reflect on what has happened and draw lessons from it.

More recent critics have seen things very differently. For Michael Scott the social world of Alicante is narrow, ignorant, hypocritical, and repressive; the play is 'an attack on the mediocrity of Alicante civilisation', and the concluding forty lines are mere 'platitudes of reconciliation' which show that the surviving characters have learned nothing from what has happened. All this enables us to see Beatrice's sin as 'one of rebellion against social regulations and propriety rather than against a spiritual concept of moral good'.[6] Peter Morrison puts the matter more forcibly:

> The essential power of the play does not lie in the complex, brainy ethics and metaphysics of mutability, but in the hollow, brooding tension between its own frightening dispassion and the blunt release of primordial violence, madness, and sexuality within an impotent, repressive, wedding-cake civilization manned by straw moralists and sanctimonious fools dressed as gentility.[7]

The main-plot characters apart from Beatrice and De Flores are 'zombies' incapable of real perception and development.

In both plots of *The Changeling* the central character is a woman. In earlier years, women critics had praised Middleton's 'supreme gift, his discernment of the minds of women', and had even seen him as 'a sympathetic defender of women'.[8] Recent feminist critics, however, have taken a much harsher view of the play, some of them finding it deeply repellent. Their arguments are often highly complex, and a brief summary is not easy. Lisa Jardine has recently argued that among the wealthier classes in the seventeenth century marriage was very much a family matter arranged to establish or consolidate networks of power and influence, and the woman's personal wishes were not considered. Beatrice undergoes a process of 'demonisation' in the play because she has the temerity to assert her own choice of partner: 'she is doomed to bring about her own destruction as soon as she woos for herself'.[9]

It might be pointed out that there are several cases in Elizabethan and Jacobean comedy of a young woman who woos for herself or successfully evades the parental choice of husband, without being either demonised or destroyed. Tragedy, however, normally portrays disaster, the failure of arrangements. In comedy the young woman usually avoids coercion by fleeing with her preferred lover, or by some relatively harmless piece of trickery; she does not arrange, as Beatrice does, for her fiancé to be murdered. The play's complicity or otherwise with patriarchy is a matter for debate. One piece of evidence that needs to be taken into account is Tomazo's speech in Act II:

> Think what a torment 'tis to marry one
> Whose heart is leapt into another's bosom;
> If ever pleasure she receive from thee,
> It comes not in thy name, or of thy gift.
> She lies but with another in thine arms . . .   (II.i.131–5)

This is obviously written from the point of view of a prospective husband; even so, it is the most powerful warning in Elizabethan drama of the dangers of forcing a woman into a loveless marriage.

It is an essential part of Jardine's argument that Alsemero should ultimately bear the blame for the disastrous course of events because he disrupts a traditional family alliance. She terms him a well-born fortune-hunter, a self-made man who in terms of the play is an interloper and adventurer.[10] The portrayal of him in the opening scene hardly seems to justify this language. Alsemero is a traveller and military man, who wanted to avenge his father's death in battle, but cannot do so because of the current truce between Spain and Holland (I.i.183–8). He is on his way to Malta; in the source from which the play is taken, but not explicitly in the play itself, this is because he wants to fight with the Knights of Malta against the Turkish enemies of Christianity. He is presumably wealthy, but we are not told how he acquired his wealth. There is nothing to hint that he is a fortune-hunter; on the contrary his friend Jasperino is amazed at his behaviour, because up to now he has shown no interest whatever in getting married.

We should also expect Beatrice's father Vermandero to regard Alsemero as a dangerous outsider who needs to be rigorously excluded. When Vermandero learns that Alsemero is from Valencia (about a hundred miles north of Alicante) he describes him as 'native' (I.i.170), or local, but when he finds out that Alsemero is the son of his old comrade-in-arms John de Alsemero he delightedly welcomes him with his 'best love' (I.i.173) and urges him to enter the castle. He comes to think so highly of Alsemero that he would be glad to incorporate him into his family: 'Valencia speaks so nobly of you, sir, / I wish I had a daughter now for you' (III.iv.1–2). At the beginning of the play he asserts that he will not accept any son-in-law other than Alonzo, but is obviously bewildered by Alonzo's sudden and inexplicable disappearance, and seems quite willing to accept Alsemero as a substitute.

Other feminist versions of the play present a more extreme position. For Sara Eaton, Beatrice is not morally culpable, because she is merely living up to male expectations of how a woman should behave. Alsemero and De Flores are the joint villains of the play, each in the end trying to silence and destroy her.[11] For Arthur Little, all the women in the play exhibit hysterical madness, forced upon them by their patriarchal community. Beatrice is broken and annihilated not by an admirable moral order but by patriarchy. De Flores' jeering at Beatrice in III.iv 'emerges as one of the misogynistic centerpieces of early modern drama', and the play as a whole 'indicts femininity as being a disease, a contagion'.[12] This is indeed a challenging view, one of whose effects is that it no longer allows us to see the play as an admirable masterpiece.[13]

Attempts have also been made to interpret the play as having political purposes: the dramatists are claimed to be attacking and satirising King James, both for his foreign policy which involved friendship with Spain and for the vicious and corrupt behaviour of his court. It is certainly true that two years later, in 1624, Middleton wrote *A Game at Chess*, the most overtly political play of the period, in which a number of leading Spaniards, as well as Spanish pretentions to world domination, were brilliantly ridiculed. But a striking point about *The Changeling*, not sufficiently recognised, is that, although it is unmistakably set in Spain, no attempt is made by the dramatists to ridicule Spain or Spanish behaviour; indeed, the Dutch, who were Protestant allies of England, are seen from a Spanish viewpoint as 'those rebellious Hollanders' (I.i.185). Furthermore, *The Changeling* is in no sense a 'court' play: it is not set in a capital city, and Vermandero is not a king but a distinguished old soldier who has been made governor of the castle in his retirement. Several characters in the main plot are of high social status but they are not given titles of nobility.

The play certainly contains what seems to be an allusion to a major scandal, the divorce trial in 1613 of Frances Howard, Countess of Essex (see the commentary on IV.i.101–2). But it is doubtful whether this should be seen as a key unlocking a wider political significance. Events in *The Changeling* bear no obvious relationship to public events in England in the early seventeenth century, and Cristina Malcolmson tries to get round this by arguing that 'the play hides its political critique of the king's policy within the contemporary debate about the proper treatment of women by their male superiors'.[14] The fullest attempt at a political reading is by Bromham and Bruzzi, but the political connections they try to establish are insubstantial and unconvincing.[15] They present Beatrice as the vicious Frances Howard, but they see De Flores as representing predatory Spanish Catholicism, so that as his intended victim Beatrice also stands for the Church of England, a virgin symbolising the pure faith of Protestantism. It is hard to see how Beatrice can project both these identities simultaneously.

FURTHER READING

The original Revels edition of *The Changeling*, which came out in 1958, was the first separate edition of the play to be published. Since then there have been several annotated editions, the most recent of which is the excellent New Mermaids version prepared by Joost Daalder (London: A. C. Black, 1990). Daalder has also written several useful essays on the play, among which are 'Folly and Madness in *The Changeling*', *Essays in Criticism*, 38 (1988), 1–21; 'The Closet Drama in *The Changeling*', *Modern Philology*, 89 (1991), 225–30; and 'The Role of Isabella in *The Changeling*', *English Studies*, 73 (1992), 22–9. The play will also be included in the new edition of the complete works of Thomas Middleton, under the general editorship of Gary Taylor, which is due to be published by the Clarendon Press, Oxford.

Distinguished earlier discussions of the play, which helped to shape attitudes towards it for much of the present century, can be found in T. S. Eliot, *Selected Essays* (see note 2); M. C. Bradbrook, *Themes and Conventions of Elizabethan Tragedy* (Cambridge: Cambridge University Press, 1935); William Empson, *Some Versions of Pastoral* (London: Chatto and Windus, 1935); and Una Ellis-Fermor, *The Jacobean Drama* (see note 8). Studies of Middleton as a dramatist often include a chapter on the play; examples are Samuel Schoenbaum, *Middleton's Tragedies: A Critical Study* (New York: Columbia University Press, 1955); Dorothy Farr, *Thomas Middleton and the Drama of Realism: A Study of Some Representative Plays* (Edinburgh: Oliver and Boyd, 1973); and Swapan Chakravorty, *Society and Politics in the Plays of Thomas Middleton* (Oxford: Clarendon Press, 1996).

There has been a great deal of criticism of *The Changeling* in the last thirty or so years, and the following list is inevitably selective. Chapters on the play can be found in a number of general or thematic studies of Jacobean drama; in some cases the title of the book gives an indication of the author's approach, as in Richard Levin's *The Multiple Plot in English Renaissance Drama* (Chicago: University of Chicago Press, 1971); Roger Stilling, *Love and Death in Renaissance Tragedy* (Baton Rouge: Louisiana State University Press, 1976); Nicholas Brooke, *Horrid Laughter in Jacobean Tragedy* (London: Open Books, 1979); T. McAlindon, *English Renaissance Tragedy* (London: Macmillan, 1986); and Martin Wiggins, *Journeymen in Murder: The Assassin in English Renaissance Drama* (Oxford: Clarendon Press, 1991).

An idea of the variety of recent critical approaches can be gained from essays which assess the play's realism. Leo Salingar, *Dramatic Form in Shakespeare and the Jacobeans* (Cambridge: Cambridge University Press, 1986), sees *The Changeling* as basically a domestic drama, and examines the skilful way in which the dramatists explore the social assumptions of the characters, especially Beatrice. Robert Jordan, however, in 'Myth and Psychology in *The Changeling*', *Renaissance Drama*, New Series 2 (1970), 157–65, argues that the play's power lies in its use of a harsh inversion of the mythical story of Beauty and the Beast. For J. L. Simmons, 'Diabolical Realism in Middleton and Rowley's *The Changeling*', *Renaissance Drama*, New Series 11 (1980), 135–70, Beatrice and De Flores are literally possessed by devils, in a way that the contemporary audience would have found plausible and convincing. Finally, Raymond Pentzell (see note 4) finds several extremely implausible features in the play, and considers that its violent shifts of tone link it with Baroque art. A useful anthology of recent criticism, selected by Roger Holdsworth, is available in the Casebook Series, *Three Jacobean Revenge Tragedies* (London: Macmillan, 1990).

NOTES

1 It has been powerfully argued that the title-page attribution of *The Spanish Gipsy* to Middleton and Rowley is mistaken or fraudulent, the play having been written by Dekker and Ford, and that Middleton and Rowley were jointly responsible for two other plays, *Wit at Several Weapons* (?1613) and *The Old Law* (?1618). See D. J. Lake, *The Canon of Middleton's Plays* (Cambridge: Cambridge University Press, 1975).

2 T. S. Eliot, 'Thomas Middleton', *Selected Essays* (London: Faber and Faber, 1932), p. 164.

3 Ricks, 'The Moral and Poetic Structure of *The Changeling*', *Essays in Criticism*, 10 (1960), 290–306.

4 Raymond J. Pentzell, '*The Changeling*: Notes on Mannerism in Dramatic

Form', in *Drama in the Renaissance*, ed. Clifford Davidson, C. J. Gianakaris, and John H. Stroupe (New York: AMS Press, 1986), pp. 282–3.

5 See Marilyn Roberts, 'A Preliminary Check-list of Productions of Thomas Middleton's Plays', *Research Opportunities in Renaissance Drama*, 28 (1985), 37–61, at 39–44.

6 Michael Scott, *Renaissance Drama and a Modern Audience* (London: Macmillan, 1982), pp. 80 and 85.

7 Peter Morrison, 'A Cangoun in Zombieland: Middleton's Teratological *Changeling*', in '*Accompaninge the Players*', *Essays Celebrating Thomas Middleton, 1580–1980*, ed. Kenneth Friedenreich (New York: AMS Press, 1983), p. 225.

8 Una Ellis-Fermor, *The Jacobean Drama* (London: Methuen, 1936), p. 149; Caroline Lockett Cherry, *The Most Unvaluedst Purchase: Women in the Plays of Thomas Middleton* (Salzburg: Institut für Englische Sprache und Literatur, 1973), p. 216.

9 Lisa Jardine, *Reading Shakespeare Historically* (London and New York: Routledge, 1996), pp. 123 and 128.

10 *Ibid.*, pp. 122–3.

11 Sara Eaton, 'Beatrice-Joanna and the Rhetoric of Love', in *Staging the Renaissance*, ed. David Scott Kastan and Peter Stallybrass (London and New York: Routledge, 1991), pp. 276 and 280.

12 Arthur L. Little, '"Transshaped" Women: Virginity and Hysteria in *The Changeling*', in *Madness in Drama*, Themes in Drama no. 15, ed. James Redmond (Cambridge: Cambridge University Press, 1993), pp. 19–42.

13 Little asserts that critics castigate Beatrice for shortcomings which are those of the play itself, *ibid.*, p. 22.

14 Cristina Malcolmson, '"As Tame as the Ladies": Politics and Gender in *The Changeling*', *English Literary Renaissance*, 20 (1990), 323. According to Malcolmson the dramatists began as radical critics, but then lost their nerve and ended up as supporters of hierarchy and patriarchy.

15 A. A. Bromham and Zara Bruzzi, *'The Changeling' and the Years of Crisis, 1619–24* (London and New York: Pinter Publishers, 1990).

THE CHANGELING

Audience are not attracted to B, more fascinated by her downfall. show her to be naive & ill-judging.

loved up,

DRAMATIS PERSONAE

ALSEMERO, *a nobleman, afterwards married to Beatrice.* *Als.*
JASPERINO, *his friend.* — *more suspicious than Als.*
BEATRICE-JOANNA, *daughter to Vermandero.* *Doesn't resist tempt a*
DIAPHANTA, *her waiting-woman.* *bad results*
VERMANDERO, *father to Beatrice.* *oblivious. proud*
DE FLORES, *servant to Vermandero.* *Scheming*
TOMAZO DE PIRACQUO, *a noble lord.* *respectable will stand b*
ALONZO DE PIRACQUO, *his brother, suitor to Beatrice.* *brother – right fo*
Servants. *innocent victim*
[Gentlemen and Gentlewomen.]

ALIBIUS, *a jealous doctor.*
LOLLIO, *his man.*
ISABELLA, *wife to Alibius.* — *resist many temptations*
ANTONIO, *the changeling.*
PEDRO, *friend to Antonio.*
FRANCISCUS, *the counterfeit madman.*
Madmen.

Mad in sane world

Scene in mad world

audience like.

SCENE: *Alicant.*

Confidants

The Changeling. 'Changeling' had various meanings in the seventeenth century. It referred in the first place to the ugly or mentally deficient child which the fairies were supposed to leave in place of a normal child which they stole. It could also refer, however, to the normal, stolen child. From these specific meanings was derived the use of the word simply as an equivalent for 'idiot', as in the play, where Antonio is 'The Changeling', though he is never referred to by this name in the actual text. Several other meanings became attached to the word—an inferior substitute, a waverer or unreliable person, and an inconstant woman—and various critics have suggested that other characters in the play, such as Beatrice, Diaphanta, and De Flores, could be considered as 'The Changeling'.

(Handwritten annotations:) Beatrice becoming more bloody sluttish as play goes on - specific moments.

The Changeling

Act I

(Handwritten: The Changeling)

(Handwritten: Main + sub-plot highlight characters mirror each other.)

[I. i]

Enter ALSEMERO.

(Handwritten: B + I)

Alsemero. 'Twas in the temple where I first beheld her,
    And now again the same; what omen yet
    Follows of that? None but imaginary.
    Why should my hopes or fate be timorous?
    The place is holy, so is my intent: 5
    I love her beauties to the holy purpose,
    And that, methinks, admits comparison
    With man's first creation, the place blest,
    And is his right home back, if he achieve it.
    The church hath first begun our interview,   10
    And that's the place must join us into one,
    So there's beginning and perfection too.

(Handwritten annotations: ironic - bea turns out v. un-holy / loves / Bea)

Enter JASPERINO.

Jasperino. Oh, sir, are you here? Come, the wind's fair with
    you.
    You're like to have a swift and pleasant passage.
Alsemero. Sure you're deceived, friend; 'tis contrary,   15
    In my best judgement.
Jasperino.   What, for Malta?

    I.i] Located at or near the harbour of Alicante, a Valencian seaport on the
east coast of Spain. This is the only outdoor scene in the play.
    6. *the holy purpose*] marriage.
    8. *the place blest*] paradise, the garden of Eden.
    9.] Marriage can restore man to his unfallen state.
    10. *interview*] sight of each other, meeting.
    12. *perfection*] bringing affairs to a perfect conclusion.
    13. *fair with you*] favourable for your departure by ship.
    14. *like*] likely.

If you could buy a gale amongst the witches,
They could not serve you such a lucky pennyworth
As comes i' God's name.

Alsemero.   Even now I observed
The temple's vane to turn full in my face;   20
I know 'tis against me.

Jasperino.   Against you?
Then you know not where you are.

Alsemero.   Not well indeed.

Jasperino. Are you not well, sir?

Alsemero.   Yes, Jasperino—
Unless there be some hidden malady
Within me that I understand not.

Jasperino.   And that   25
I begin to doubt, sir; I never knew
Your inclinations to travels at a pause
With any cause to hinder it, till now.
Ashore you were wont to call your servants up,
And help to trap your horses for the speed.   30
At sea I have seen you weigh the anchor with 'em,
Hoist sails for fear to lose the foremost breath,
Be in continual prayers for fair winds;
And have you changed your orisons?

Alsemero.   No, friend,
I keep the same church, same devotion.   35

Jasperino. Lover I'm sure you're none; the stoic was
Found in you long ago; your mother nor
Best friends, who have set snares of beauty (ay,

---

17. *buy . . . witches*] Witches were thought to control the winds, and could sell a favourable wind to seamen.

18. *pennyworth*] bargain.

19. *i' God's name*] a stock phrase meaning 'free, for nothing' (perhaps with a hint that God is telling Alsemero to go).

20. *vane*] weather vane, showing wind direction.

22–3. *Not well . . . not well*] This play on words is characteristic of Rowley; compare I.ii.19–20 and V.iii.16.

26. *doubt*] fear, suspect.

30. *trap*] put on trappings or harness.
for the speed] to hasten matters.

31. *'em*] the sailors.

34. *orisons*] prayers.

And choice ones, too), could never trap you that way.
What might be the cause?
Alsemero.   Lord, how violent   40
Thou art! I was but meditating of
Somewhat I heard within the temple.
Jasperino. Is this violence? 'Tis but idleness
Compared with your haste yesterday.
Alsemero. I'm all this while a-going, man.   45

Enter Servants.

Jasperino. Backwards, I think, sir. Look, your servants.
1 Servant. The seamen call. Shall we board your trunks?
Alsemero. No, not today.
Jasperino. 'Tis the critical day, it seems, and the sign in
Aquarius.   50
2 Servant. [*Aside*] We must not to sea today; this smoke will
bring forth fire.
Alsemero. Keep all on shore; I do not know the end
(Which needs I must do) of an affair in hand
Ere I can go to sea.   55
1 Servant. Well, your pleasure.
2 Servant. [*Aside*] Let him e'en take his leisure too; we are
safer on land.   *Exeunt* Servants.

Enter BEATRICE-JOANNA, DIAPHANTA, *and* Servants.
[*Alsemero greets Beatrice and kisses her.*]

Jasperino. [*Aside*] How now! The laws of the Medes are
changed sure; salute a woman? He kisses too; wonderful!   60
Where learnt he this? And does it perfectly too; in my
conscience he ne'er rehearsed it before. Nay, go on, this

---

42. *Somewhat*] something.

47. *board*] put on board.

49. *critical*] crucial, decisive (a term used in astrology and medicine).

49–50. *sign in Aquarius*] indicating that the time is propitious for travel by water.

51–2. *this . . . fire*] this will have serious consequences (based on the proverb, 'no smoke without fire').

56. *your pleasure*] as you wish.

59. *laws of the Medes*] laws which remained unchanged (Daniel, 6.8).

60. *salute*] greet.

61–2. *in my conscience*] i.e. on my word, truly (hinting at surprise and incredulity).

will be stranger and better news at Valencia than if he had
ransomed half Greece from the Turk.

Beatrice. You are a scholar, sir?

Alsemero.   A weak one, lady.   65

Beatrice. Which of the sciences is this love you speak of?

Alsemero. From your tongue I take it to be music.

Beatrice. You are skilful in't, can sing at first sight.

Alsemero. And I have showed you all my skill at once.
      I want more words to express me further,   70
      And must be forced to repetition:
      I love you dearly.

Beatrice.   Be better advised, sir.
      Our eyes are sentinels unto our judgements,
      And should give certain judgement what they see;
      But they are rash sometimes and tell us wonders   75
      Of common things, which when our judgements find,
      They can then check the eyes and call them blind.

Alsemero. But I am further, lady; yesterday
      Was mine eyes' employment, and hither now
      They brought my judgement, where are both agreed.   80
      Both houses then consenting, 'tis agreed;
      Only there wants the confirmation
      By the hand royal. That's your part, lady.

Beatrice. Oh, there's one above me, sir. [*Aside*] For five
            days past
      To be recalled! Sure, mine eyes were mistaken;   85
      This was the man was meant me. That he should come
      So near his time, and miss it!

---

64. *ransomed . . . Turk*] Greece at this time was part of the Turkish empire,
not achieving freedom until the nineteenth century.

66. *sciences*] learning in general (not exclusively 'scientific').

68. *sing at first sight*] (1) sight-read the music immediately; (2) talk of love
as soon as you see a woman.

70. *want*] lack, need.

76. *find*] find out, perceive.

77. *check*] restrain, rebuke.

78. *further*] at a further stage (he has completed and gone beyond what
Beatrice has told him to do).

81. *Both houses*] the two houses of parliament (in this case 'eyes' and
'judgement').

82–3.] The bill needs only the royal signature to become law.

84. *one above me*] Vermandero, or possibly God.

five days past] Presumably Beatrice was betrothed to Alonzo five days ago.

Jasperino. [*Aside*] We might have come by the carriers from
　　Valencia, I see, and saved all our sea-provision; we are at
　　farthest, sure. Methinks I should do something too;　　　90
　　I meant to be a venturer in this voyage.
　　Yonder's another vessel; I'll board her.
　　If she be lawful prize, down goes her top-sail.
　　　　　　　　　　　　[*He greets Diaphanta.*]

　　　　　　　　Enter DE FLORES.

De Flores. Lady, your father—
Beatrice.　　　　　　　Is in health, I hope.
De Flores. Your eye shall instantly instruct you, lady.　　　95
　　He's coming hitherward.
Beatrice.　　　　　　　What needed then
　　Your duteous preface? I had rather
　　He had come unexpected; you must stall
　　A good presence with unnecessary blabbing.
　　And how welcome for your part you are,　　　　　100
　　I'm sure you know.
De Flores. [*Aside*]　　Will't never mend, this scorn,
　　One side nor other? Must I be enjoined
　　To follow still whilst she flies from me? Well,
　　Fates do your worst; I'll please myself with sight
　　Of her, at all opportunities,　　　　　　　　105
　　If but to spite her anger. I know she had
　　Rather see me dead than living, and yet
　　She knows no cause for't but a peevish will.
Alsemero. You seemed displeased, lady, on the sudden.
Beatrice. Your pardon, sir, 'tis my infirmity,　　　　　110
　　Nor can I other reason render you

---

88. *the carriers*] transport by land rather than sea.

89–90. *at farthest*] farthest away from the goal, least successful.

91. *venturer*] someone who shares the risks and profits of a commercial
voyage.

92. *board*] capture by going on board, i.e. accost, strike up a conversation.

93. *lawful prize*] a legitimate target (an unmarried woman).

down . . . top-sail] she will soon lower her sails, in token of surrender.

98. *stall*] anticipate, forestall.

99. *A good presence*] that of my father, whose dignity is lessened by your
'blabbing'.

102. *One . . . other*] one way or another.

Than his or hers, of some particular thing
They must abandon as a deadly poison,
Which to a thousand other tastes were wholesome.
Such to mine eyes is that same fellow there,   115
The same that report speaks of the basilisk.

Alsemero. This is a frequent frailty in our nature.
There's scarce a man amongst a thousand sound
But hath his imperfection: one distastes
The scent of roses, which to infinites   120
Most pleasing is, and odoriferous;
One oil, the enemy of poison;
Another wine, the cheerer of the heart
And lively refresher of the countenance.
Indeed this fault (if so it be) is general,   125
There's scarce a thing but is both loved and loathed.
Myself, I must confess, have the same frailty.

Beatrice. And what may be your poison, sir? I am bold with
      you.

Alsemero. What might be your desire, perhaps, a cherry.

Beatrice. I am no enemy to any creature   130
My memory has but yon gentleman.

Alsemero. He does ill to tempt your sight, if he knew it.

---

112. *his or hers*] reasons put forward by any other man or woman.

116. *report*] rumour, generally accepted belief.

the basilisk] a fabulous beast that could kill by a glance.

118. *sound*] healthy.

119. *imperfection*] not illness, but psychological quirk. Even among a thousand sound or healthy people, who might be expected not to display oddities of temperament, there is scarcely one who does not have a strong antipathy towards some object or person which cannot be rationally justified.

distastes] dislikes.

120. *infinites*] infinite numbers of people.

121. *odoriferous*] fragrant, sweet-smelling.

122.] Someone dislikes oil, which can be used as an antidote to poison.

122–4.] perhaps an echo of Psalm 104.15, 'wine that maketh glad the heart of man, and oil to make his face to shine'.

129.] I dislike cherries, which you may perhaps be fond of.

131. *My memory has*] that I hold in my memory.

132.] De Flores does wrong to appear before you, if he knows of your displeasure.

Beatrice. He cannot be ignorant of that, sir.
    I have not spared to tell him so; and I want
    To help myself, since he's a gentleman   135
    In good respect with my father, and follows him.
Alsemero. He's out of his place then now.

                                    [*They talk apart.*]

Jasperino. [*To Diaphanta*] I am a mad wag, wench.
Diaphanta. So methinks; but for your comfort I can tell
    you, we have a doctor in the city that undertakes the   140
    cure of such.
Jasperino. Tush, I know what physic is best for the state of
    mine own body.
Diaphanta. 'Tis scarce a well-governed state, I believe.
Jasperino. I could show thee such a thing with an ingredient 145
    that we two would compound together, and if it did not
    tame the maddest blood i' th' town for two hours after I'll
    ne'er profess physic again.
Diaphanta. A little poppy, sir, were good to cause you sleep.
Jasperino. Poppy! I'll give thee a pop i' th' lips for that first, 150
    and begin there. [*He kisses her.*] Poppy is one simple
    indeed, and cuckoo what you call't another. I'll discover

---

134–6. *and . . . him*] i.e. I am unable to do anything about it because my
father likes and employs him.

137. *out of his place*] (1) not in the right place, as he should keep away from
you; (2) not behaving as a servant should.

138. *mad wag*] high-spirited and playful person (but Diaphanta interprets
'mad' literally).

140. *doctor*] Alibius.

142. *physic*] medicine (but Jasperino's speeches here are full of sexual
innuendoes).

144. *a well-governed state*] (1) in a healthy condition; (2) an orderly
kingdom.

146. *compound*] mix, combine (in the act of copulation).

148. *profess physic*] claim to have medical knowledge.

149. *poppy*] opium.

150. *pop*] kiss (playing on the first syllable of 'poppy').

151. *simple*] herb or drug.

152. *cuckoo what you call't*] There are various types of cuckoo flower; this
seems to refer primarily to the wild or common arum, wake-robin, known
also as cuckoo-pintle because it produces thick fleshy spikes resembling a
penis.

discover] reveal.

no more now; another time I'll show thee all.
Beatrice. My father, sir.

Enter VERMANDERO *and* Servants.

Vermandero. Oh, Joanna, I came to meet thee.   155
    Your devotion's ended?
Beatrice.   For this time, sir.
    [*Aside*] I shall change my saint, I fear me; I find
    A giddy turning in me. [*To Vermandero*] Sir, this while
    I am beholding to this gentleman,
    Who left his own way to keep me company,   160
    And in discourse I find him much desirous
    To see your castle. He hath deserved it, sir,
    If ye please to grant it.
Vermandero.   With all my heart, sir.
    Yet there's an article between; I must know
    Your country. We use not to give survey   165
    Of our chief strengths to strangers; our citadels
    Are placed conspicuous to outward view
    On promonts' tops, but within are secrets.
Alsemero. A Valencian, sir.
Vermandero.   A Valencian?
    That's native, sir; of what name, I beseech you?   170
Alsemero. Alsemero, sir.
Vermandero.   Alsemero; not the son
    Of John de Alsemero?
Alsemero.   The same, sir.
Vermandero. My best love bids you welcome.

---

   153. *show thee all*] tell you everything (with an obscene implication).

   157. *change my saint*] (1) adopt a new patron saint; (2) find a new lover
(compare V.iii.53).

   159. *beholding*] indebted.

   164. *article between*] condition which must be fulfilled first.

   165. *use not*] are not accustomed.

   166. *strengths*] fortifications.

   168. *promonts'*] promontories'.

   secrets] Vermandero is concerned about military security, but his remark is
ironic (there are more secrets than he realises).

Beatrice. [*Aside*]   He was wont
    To call me so, and then he speaks a most
    Unfeignèd truth.
Vermandero.   Oh, sir, I knew your father;   175
    We two were in acquaintance long ago,
    Before our chins were worth Iulan down,
    And so continued till the stamp of time
    Had coined us into silver. Well, he's gone;
    A good soldier went with him.   180
Alsemero. You went together in that, sir.
Vermandero. No, by Saint Jacques, I came behind him.
    Yet I have done somewhat too. An unhappy day
    Swallowed him at last at Gibraltar
    In fight with those rebellious Hollanders;   185
    Was it not so?
Alsemero.   Whose death I had revenged,
    Or followed him in fate, had not the late league
    Prevented me.
Vermandero.   Ay, ay, 'twas time to breathe.—
    Oh, Joanna, I should ha' told thee news:
    I saw Piracquo lately.
Beatrice. [*Aside*]   That's ill news.   190

173–5.] Vermandero's phrase means 'I give you a loving welcome'. In her aside Beatrice notes that he also used to refer to her as 'my best love', and if, in using the phrase now, he means that Beatrice bids Alsemero welcome, he is certainly speaking the truth.

177.] i.e. before our beards began to grow. 'Iulan' does not occur elsewhere; it probably derives from Iulus Ascanius, the son of Aeneas in Virgil's *Aeneid*, whose name was thought to come from a Greek word meaning 'the first growth of the beard'.

179. *Had . . . silver*] i.e. had turned our beards grey.

181.] i.e. Vermandero and Alsemero's father were equally good soldiers.

182. *Saint Jacques*] St James the Greater, the patron saint of Spain.

184. *Gibraltar*] The naval battle of Gibraltar, in which the Dutch fleet gained a decisive victory over a larger Spanish fleet, took place on 25 April 1607.

187. *the late league*] The treaty of The Hague was signed on 9 April 1609, and provided for a truce of hostilities between Spain and the Netherlands lasting twelve years.

188. *Prevented*] forestalled.

breathe] pause from fighting to recover one's breath.

Vermandero. He's hot preparing for this day of triumph;
    Thou must be a bride within this sevennight.
Alsemero. [*Aside*]   Ha!
Beatrice. [*To Vermandero*] Nay, good sir, be not so violent;
      with speed
    I cannot render satisfaction
    Unto the dear companion of my soul,   195
    Virginity, whom I thus long have lived with,
    And part with it so rude and suddenly.
    Can such friends divide, never to meet again,
    Without a solemn farewell?
Vermandero.   Tush, tush, there's a toy.
Alsemero. [*Aside*] I must now part, and never meet again   200
    With any joy on earth. [*To Vermandero*] Sir, your pardon.
    My affairs call on me.
Vermandero.   How, sir? By no means;
    Not changed so soon, I hope? You must see my castle,
    And her best entertainment, ere we part;
    I shall think myself unkindly used else.   205
    Come, come, let's on. I had good hope your stay
    Had been a while with us in Alicant;
    I might have bid you to my daughter's wedding.
Alsemero. [*Aside*] He means to feast me, and poisons me
      beforehand.
    [*To Vermandero*] I should be dearly glad to be there, sir,   210
    Did my occasions suit as I could wish.
Beatrice. I shall be sorry if you be not there
    When it is done, sir—but not so suddenly.
Vermandero. I tell you, sir, the gentleman's complete,
    A courtier and a gallant, enriched   215
    With many fair and noble ornaments.
    I would not change him for a son-in-law
    For any he in Spain, the proudest he,
    And we have great ones, that you know.
Alsemero.   He's much

---

    199. *toy*] trifling objection.
    214. *complete*] possessing all the skills and accomplishments appropriate to
a gentleman.
    217. *change*] exchange.

Bound to you, sir.

Vermandero.   He shall be bound to me,   220

As fast as this tie can hold him; I'll want

My will else.

Beatrice. [*Aside*] I shall want mine if you do it.

Vermandero. But come, by the way I'll tell you more of him.

Alsemero. [*Aside*] How shall I dare to venture in his castle,

When he discharges murderers at the gate? —   225

But I must on, for back I cannot go.

Beatrice. [*Aside*] Not this serpent gone yet?

                                        [*She drops a glove.*]

Vermandero.   Look, girl, thy glove's fall'n;

Stay, stay.—De Flores, help a little.

                  [*Exeunt* VERMANDERO, ALSEMERO, JASPERINO,

                                        and Servants.]

De Flores.   Here, lady. [*He offers the glove.*]

Beatrice. Mischief on your officious forwardness!

Who bade you stoop? They touch my hand no more.   230

There, for t'other's sake I part with this.

        [*She takes off the other glove and throws it down.*]

Take 'em and draw thine own skin off with 'em.

                  Exeunt [BEATRICE-JOANNA *and* DIAPHANTA].

De Flores. Here's a favour come, with a mischief! Now I know

She had rather wear my pelt tanned in a pair

Of dancing pumps than I should thrust my fingers   235

Into her sockets here, I know she hates me,

---

220. *Bound . . . bound*] (1) indebted, obliged; (2) tied.

221–2. *I'll want . . . else*] otherwise I shall not get what I want (implying that Vermandero is stubbornly determined to get his own way).

225. *murderers*] small cannon (a grim dramatic irony; see Introduction, p. 6).

227 S.D.] It is not clear whether Beatrice drops the glove accidentally, or deliberately for Alsemero to pick up. It is unlikely that, as some critics suggest, she is unconsciously offering it to De Flores.

229. *Mischief*] an expletive ('may evil befall you').

232. *thine own skin*] perhaps a scornful allusion to the disfiguring skin disease from which De Flores suffers.

233. *favour*] love token (spoken ironically).

Now I know] i.e. although, even though, I know. It is not an adverb of time; he has long known of her aversion.

235. *pumps*] slippers, shoes for dancing.

236. *sockets*] the fingers of the glove (the idea of thrusting fingers into sockets clearly has sexual overtones).

Yet cannot choose but love her.

No matter; if but to vex her, I'll haunt her still.

Though I get nothing else, I'll have my will.   *Exit.*

[I. ii]

Enter ALIBIUS *and* LOLLIO.

Alibius. Lollio, I must trust thee with a secret,

    But thou must keep it.

Lollio. I was ever close to a secret, sir.

Alibius. The diligence that I have found in thee,

    The care and industry already past,   5

    Assures me of thy good continuance.

    Lollio, I have a wife.

Lollio. Fie, sir, 'tis too late to keep her secret; she's known to

    be married all the town and country over.

Alibius. Thou goest too fast, my Lollio. That knowledge,   10

    I allow, no man can be barred it;

    But there is a knowledge which is nearer,

    Deeper and sweeter, Lollio.

Lollio. Well, sir, let us handle that between you and I.

Alibius. 'Tis that I go about, man. Lollio,   15

    My wife is young.

Lollio. So much the worse to be kept secret, sir.

Alibius. Why, now thou meet'st the substance of the point:

    I am old, Lollio.

Lollio. No, sir, 'tis I am old Lollio.   20

Alibius. Yet why may not this concord and sympathise?

    Old trees and young plants often grow together,

    Well enough agreeing.

Lollio. Ay, sir, but the old trees raise themselves higher and

    broader than the young plants.   25

I.ii] This and all subsequent sub-plot scenes are located in a room in Alibius's madhouse.

3. *close*] reticent, given to concealment.

14. *handle*] discuss (but also implying that he would like to have sexual knowledge of Isabella).

15. *'Tis . . . about*] That's what I'm talking about.

21. *this*] a marriage between an old man and young woman.

24–5.] implying that Alibius may grow taller through having to wear the cuckold's horns.

Alibius. Shrewd application! There's the fear, man;
    I would wear my ring on my own finger.
    Whilst it is borrowed it is none of mine,
    But his that useth it.

Lollio. You must keep it on still then; if it but lie by, one or   30
    other will be thrusting into't.

Alibius. Thou conceiv'st me, Lollio. Here thy watchful eye
    Must have employment; I cannot always be
    At home.

Lollio. I dare swear you cannot.   35

Alibius. I must look out.

Lollio. I know't, you must look out, 'tis every man's case.

Alibius. Here I do say must thy employment be,
    To watch her treadings and in my absence
    Supply my place.   40

Lollio. I'll do my best, sir, yet surely I cannot see who you
    should have cause to be jealous of.

Alibius. Thy reason for that, Lollio? 'Tis a comfortable
    question.

Lollio. We have but two sorts of people in the house, and both   45
    under the whip, that's fools and madmen; the one has not
    wit enough to be knaves, and the other not knavery
    enough to be fools.

Alibius. Ay, those are all my patients, Lollio.
    I do profess the cure of either sort;   50
    My trade, my living 'tis, I thrive by it.
    But here's the care that mixes with my thrift:
    The daily visitants, that come to see
    My brainsick patients, I would not have

---

26. *Shrewd application*] Lollio's remark has a painful significance.

27.] (1) I wish to continue to wear my wedding ring; (2) I wish to keep safe my wife's married chastity. (*Ring* suggests his wife's vagina.)

32. *conceiv'st*] understand.

37. *'tis . . . case*] it is true for every man.

39. *treadings*] movements, actions.

40. *Supply my place*] act as my substitute (Alibius means only that Lollio should watch over her, but the phrase has an unintended sexual meaning).

43. *comfortable*] reassuring, comforting.

53. *daily visitants*] Bethlehem Hospital, a famous asylum of the time, was regarded as a place of entertainment by the citizens of London, who went to it to be amused by the antics of the inmates.

To see my wife. Gallants I do observe   55
Of quick enticing eyes, rich in habits,
Of stature and proportion very comely;
These are most shrewd temptations, Lollio.

Lollio. They may be easily answered, sir; if they come to see
the fools and madmen, you and I may serve the turn, and   60
let my mistress alone; she's of neither sort.

Alibius. 'Tis a good ward; indeed come they to see
Our madmen or our fools. Let 'em see no more
Than what they come for; by that consequent
They must not see her. I'm sure she's no fool.   65

Lollio. And I'm sure she's no madman.

Alibius. Hold that buckler fast, Lollio; my trust
Is on thee, and I account it firm and strong.
What hour is't, Lollio?

Lollio. Towards belly-hour, sir.   70

Alibius. Dinner time? Thou mean'st twelve o'clock.

Lollio. Yes, sir, for every part has his hour: we wake at six and
look about us, that's eye-hour; at seven we should pray,
that's knee-hour; at eight walk, that's leg-hour; at nine
gather flowers and pluck a rose, that's nose-hour; at ten   75
we drink, that's mouth-hour; at eleven lay about us for
victuals, that's hand-hour; at twelve go to dinner, that's
belly-hour.

Alibius. Profoundly, Lollio! It will be long
Ere all thy scholars learn this lesson, and   80
I did look to have a new one entered.—Stay,
I think my expectation is come home.

---

56. *habits*] clothes.

58. *shrewd*] powerful, mischievous.

60. *serve the turn*] be sufficient (but with a joking implication that Lollio
and Alibius are fools or madmen).

62. *ward*] position of defence in fencing.

indeed come they] they certainly come.

64. *consequent*] logical deduction.

67. *Hold . . . fast*] Keep the fact that Isabella is neither fool nor madwoman
firmly in mind as a means of protecting her. (A *buckler* is a shield.)

75. *pluck a rose*] possibly intended literally, but also a slang phrase for
urinating.

76. *lay about us*] search vigorously.

82.] (1) what I expected has happened; (2) my new patient has arrived.

Enter PEDRO, *and* ANTONIO *like an idiot.*

Pedro. Save you, sir. My business speaks itself;
  This sight takes off the labour of my tongue.

Alibius. Ay, ay, sir;   85
  'Tis plain enough, you mean him for my patient.

Pedro. And if your pains prove but commodious, to give but
  some little strength to his sick and weak part of nature in
  him, these are [*Giving money*] but patterns to show you of
  the whole pieces that will follow to you, beside the charge   90
  of diet, washing, and other necessaries fully defrayed.

Alibius. Believe it, sir, there shall no care be wanting.

Lollio. Sir, an officer in this place may deserve something; the
  trouble will pass through my hands.

Pedro. 'Tis fit something should come to your hands then, sir.   95
                                         [*He gives him money.*]

Lollio. Yes, sir, 'tis I must keep him sweet, and read to him.
  What is his name?

Pedro. His name is Antonio; marry, we use but half to him,
  only Tony.

Lollio. Tony, Tony, 'tis enough, and a very good name for a   100
  fool.—What's your name, Tony?

Antonio. He, he, he! Well, I thank you, cousin; he, he, he!

Lollio. Good boy! Hold up your head.—He can laugh; I perceive by that he is no beast.

Pedro. Well, sir,   105
  If you can raise him but to any height,

82.1. *like an idiot*] The frontispiece to *The Wits, or Sport upon Sport*, a collection of drolls published by Francis Kirkman in 1672, shows various stage characters including 'Changeling'. The figure wears a voluminous coat or gown with long sleeves and skirts, and a tall conical hat with no brim. From his wrist dangles a rectangular object that may be a horn-book.

83. *Save you*] God save you (a greeting).

87. *commodious*] beneficial.

89. *patterns*] samples.

90. *whole pieces*] large and valuable coins.

charge] expenses (payment had to be made when a new patient was brought to Bethlehem Hospital).

96. *sweet*] clean.

99. *Tony*] In the later seventeenth century 'tony' was sometimes used to mean 'fool', a usage probably deriving from this play.

103–4. *laugh ... no beast*] The doctrine that humans are distinguished from other beasts by the faculty of laughter derives ultimately from Aristotle.

Any degree of wit, might he attain
(As I might say) to creep but on all four
Towards the chair of wit, or walk on crutches,
'Twould add an honour to your worthy pains,   110
And a great family might pray for you,
To which he should be heir, had he discretion
To claim and guide his own. Assure you, sir,
He is a gentleman.

Lollio. Nay, there's nobody doubted that; at first sight I knew   115
him for a gentleman. He looks no other yet.

Pedro. Let him have good attendance and sweet lodging.

Lollio. As good as my mistress lies in, sir; and as you allow us
time and means, we can raise him to the higher degree of
discretion.   120

Pedro. Nay, there shall no cost want, sir.

Lollio. He will hardly be stretched up to the wit of a
magnifico.

Pedro. Oh, no, that's not to be expected; far shorter will be
enough.   125

Lollio. I'll warrant you I make him fit to bear office in five
weeks; I'll undertake to wind him up to the wit of
constable.

Pedro. If it be lower than that it might serve turn.

Lollio. No, fie, to level him with a headborough, beadle, or   130
watchman were but little better than he is. Constable I'll
able him; if he do come to be a justice afterwards, let him
thank the keeper. Or I'll go further with you; say I do
bring him up to my own pitch, say I make him as wise as
myself.   135

115–16.] Does this mean that Lollio sees through Antonio's disguise at the
very beginning?

118. *As good . . . lies in*] perhaps again hinting that Lollio understands
Antonio's purpose towards Isabella.

121.] All expenses will be paid; don't stint.

123. *magnifico*] a magistrate of Venice; in this context, a senior judge or
legal official.

127–8. *wit of constable*] Constables were regularly regarded as stupid, and
played as figures of fun on the Elizabethan stage.

130. *headborough*] a parish officer with duties similar to that of constable.
beadle] minor parish officer who assisted the constable.

132. *able him*] make him fit for.

Pedro. Why, there I would have it.

Lollio. Well, go to, either I'll be as arrant a fool as he or he
  shall be as wise as I, and then I think 'twill serve his turn.

Pedro. Nay, I do like thy wit passing well.

Lollio. Yes, you may. Yet if I had not been a fool, I had had   140
  more wit than I have too; remember what state you find
  me in.

Pedro. I will, and so leave you; your best cares, I beseech you.

Alibius. Take you none with you; leave 'em all with us.

                                              Exit PEDRO.

Antonio. Oh, my cousin's gone. Cousin, cousin, oh!   145

Lollio. Peace, peace, Tony, you must not cry, child, you must
  be whipped if you do. Your cousin is here still; I am your
  cousin, Tony.

Antonio. He, he! Then I'll not cry, if thou be'st my cousin, he,
  he, he!   150

Lollio. [*To Alibius*] I were best try his wit a little, that I may
  know what form to place him in.

Alibius. Ay, do, Lollio, do.

Lollio. I must ask him easy questions at first.—Tony, how
  many true fingers has a tailor on his right hand?   155

Antonio. As many as on his left, cousin.

Lollio. Good; and how many on both?

Antonio. Two less than a deuce, cousin.

Lollio. Very well answered. I come to you again, cousin Tony:
  how many fools goes to a wise man?   160

---

137. *go to*] an expression of remonstrance.

139. *passing*] extremely.

140–2.] perhaps implying that if Lollio had been more intelligent he would
have found himself a better job.

141. *state*] as a keeper of fools and madmen.

143. *your best cares*] take the utmost care in treating Antonio (but in his
reply Lollio puns on *cares* as 'worries, responsibilities').

151. *try*] test.

152. *form*] class in school.

155. *true*] honest.

tailor] Tailors were proverbially thought to be dishonest, and to steal cloth
from customers when making up garments.

158.] i.e. none at all.

160. *goes to*] (1) make up, constitute; (2) visit. Lollio intends the first sense;
Antonio takes it in the second. (The use of a singular verb with a plural
subject was normal in the period.)

Antonio. Forty in a day sometimes, cousin.

Lollio. Forty in a day? How prove you that?

Antonio. All that fall out amongst themselves and go to a
lawyer to be made friends.

Lollio. A parlous fool! He must sit in the fourth form at least,   165
I perceive that. I come again, Tony: how many knaves
make an honest man?

Antonio. I know not that, cousin.

Lollio. No, the question is too hard for you. I'll tell you,
cousin, there's three knaves may make an honest man: a   170
sergeant, a jailor, and a beadle; the sergeant catches him,
the jailor holds him, and the beadle lashes him; and if he
be not honest then, the hangman must cure him.

Antonio. Ha, ha ha, that's fine sport, cousin!

Alibius. This was too deep a question for the fool, Lollio.   175

Lollio. Yes, this might have served yourself, though I say't.—
Once more, and you shall go play, Tony.

Antonio. Ay, play at push-pin, cousin, ha, he!

Lollio. So thou shalt. Say how many fools are here—

Antonio. Two, cousin, thou and I.   180

Lollio. Nay, you're too forward there, Tony. Mark my question: how many fools and knaves are here? A fool before
a knave, a fool behind a knave, between every two fools a
knave; how many fools, how many knaves?

Antonio. I never learnt so far, cousin.   185

Alibius. Thou putt'st too hard questions to him, Lollio.

Lollio. I'll make him understand it easily. Cousin, stand there.

Antonio. Ay, cousin.

     [*Lollio arranges them in a row, Alibius in the middle.*]

Lollio. Master, stand you next the fool.

163–4.] i.e. They are fools to expect a lawyer to reconcile them, because a
lawyer thrives on litigation. The status of the lawyer as a 'wise man' is heavily
ironic.

165. *parlous*] sly, cunning.

167. *make*] (1) make up; (2) create.

176. *served*] been appropriate to (perhaps insinuating that Alibius himself
would not have solved the problem).

178. *push-pin*] a childish game played with small pins (but with an obscene
implication).

182. *before*] in front of.

187ff.] Alibius in the middle is the knave between two fools. The others are
really the knaves who are trying to make a fool of Alibius.

Alibius. Well, Lollio?   190

Lollio. Here's my place. Mark now, Tony: there a fool before
    a knave.

Antonio. That's I, cousin.

Lollio. Here's a fool behind a knave, that's I, and between us
    two fools there is a knave, that's my master; 'tis but we   195
    three, that's all.

Antonio. We three, we three, cousin!   *Madmen within.*

1. (*Within*) Put's head i' th' pillory! The bread's too little.

2. (*Within*) Fly, fly, and he catches the swallow.

3. (*Within*) Give her more onion, or the devil put the rope   200
    about her crag.

Lollio. You may hear what time of day it is; the chimes of
    Bedlam goes.

Alibius. Peace, peace, or the wire comes!

3. (*Within*) Cat-whore, cat-whore, her permasant, her   205
    permasant!

Alibius. Peace, I say!—Their hour's come; they must be fed,
    Lollio.

Lollio. There's no hope of recovery of that Welsh madman,
    was undone by a mouse, that spoiled him a permasant;   210
    lost his wits for't.

Alibius. Go to your charge, Lollio, I'll to mine.

Lollio. Go you to your madmen's ward; let me alone with
    your fools.

---

191. *before*] in front of.

195–6. *we three*] a stock joke in which a picture of two fools is labelled 'we
three', the third being the spectator.

198ff.] The references to food in the madmen's speeches suggest that they
are not adequately fed.

200. *rope*] (1) hangman's rope; (2) rope of onions.

200–1. *her*] stage-Welsh for 'me' and 'my'.

201. *crag*] neck.

202–3. *chimes of Bedlam*] cries of the inmates for food. 'Bedlam' is an
abbreviation of Bethlehem Hospital (though Rowley is not offering a realistic
portrayal of it).

204. *wire*] whip made of wire.

205–6.] Apparently the Welsh madman is reviling his cat for failing to
protect his Parmesan cheese.

209–10.] The fondness of the Welsh for cheese was proverbial in Elizabethan England.

210. *was*] who was.

212. *charge*] those you are in charge of (the fools).

Alibius. And remember my last charge, Lollio.   215
Lollio. Of which your patients do you think I am?—Come,
     Tony, you must amongst your school-fellows now.
     There's pretty scholars amongst 'em, I can tell you;
     there's some of 'em at *stultus, stulta, stultum*.
Antonio. I would see the madmen, cousin, if they would not   220
     bite me.
Lollio. No, they shall not bite thee, Tony.
Antonio. They bite when they are at dinner, do they not, coz?
Lollio. They bite at dinner indeed, Tony. Well, I hope to get
     credit by thee. I like thee the best of all the scholars that   225
     ever I brought up, and thou shalt prove a wise man or I'll
     prove a fool myself.   *Exeunt*.

---

215. *charge*] instruction (to keep watch on the madmen and Isabella).
219.] They have mastered the three genders of the Latin word for 'foolish'.
223. *coz*] abbreviation of 'cousin'.

Act II

[II. i]

Enter BEATRICE-JOANNA *and* JASPERINO *severally.*

Beatrice. Oh, sir, I'm ready now for that fair service
    Which makes the name of friend sit glorious on you.
    Good angels and this conduct be your guide!
                         [*She gives a paper.*]
    Fitness of time and place is there set down, sir.
Jasperino. The joy I shall return rewards my service.   *Exit.*   5
Beatrice. How wise is Alsemero in his friend!
    It is a sign he makes his choice with judgement.
    Then I appear in nothing more approved
    Than making choice of him;
    For 'tis a principle, he that can choose   10
    That bosom well, who of his thoughts partakes,
    Proves most discreet in every choice he makes.
    Methinks I love now with the eyes of judgement,
    And see the way to merit, clearly see it.
    A true deserver like a diamond sparkles;   15
    In darkness you may see him, that's in absence,
    Which is the greatest darkness falls on love;
    Yet is he best discernèd then
    With intellectual eyesight. What's Piracquo
    My father spends his breath for? And his blessing   20

II.i] This and all subsequent main-plot scenes are located inside Vermandero's castle.

0.1. severally] separately.

3. *conduct*] paper giving directions.

5. *return*] i.e. take back to Alsemero.

8. *approved*] justified.

11. *bosom*] intimate friend.

15–16.] Diamonds were supposed to be luminous; compare III.ii.20–3.

17. *falls*] that falls.

20. *My . . . for*] on whose behalf my father speaks at length.

his blessing] my father's; he will not bless me unless I marry well and maintain the family reputation ('his name', line 21).

Is only mine as I regard his name;
Else it goes from me and turns head against me,
Transformed into a curse. Some speedy way
Must be remembered. He's so forward too,
So urgent that way, scarce allows me breath   25
To speak to my new comforts.

Enter DE FLORES.

De Flores. [*Aside*]   Yonder's she.
Whatever ails me, now alate especially?
I can as well be hanged as refrain seeing her.
Some twenty times a day—nay, not so little—
Do I force errands, frame ways and excuses   30
To come into her sight, and I have small reason for't
And less encouragement; for she baits me still
Every time worse than other, does profess herself
The cruellest enemy to my face in town;
At no hand can abide the sight of me,   35
As if danger or ill luck hung in my looks.
I must confess my face is bad enough,
But I know far worse has better fortune,
And not endured alone, but doted on;
And yet such pick-haired faces, chins like witches',   40
Here and there five hairs, whispering in a corner,
As if they grew in fear one of another,
Wrinkles like troughs, where swine-deformity swills
The tears of perjury that lie there like wash

---

22. *turns head against*] turns round and attacks.

24. *remembered*] thought of, brought to mind.
forward] eager.

26. *comforts*] i.e. Alsemero; compare II.ii.32.

27. *alate*] of late, recently.

30. *force*] invent (with a hint that he forces himself into her presence).
frame] devise.

32. *baits*] harasses, torments (as in bull- or bear-baiting).

35. *At no hand*] by no means.

35–6.] Compare II.i.89–90 and V.iii.154–7.

40. *pick-haired*] with hard, bristly hairs.

43–4. *swine-deformity . . . perjury*] pig-like ugliness swallows down the hypocritical tears.

44. *wash*] (1) watery discharge; (2) liquid food for pigs.

Fallen from the slimy and dishonest eye—   45
Yet such a one plucked sweets without restraint
And has the grace of beauty to his sweet.
Though my hard fate has thrust me out to servitude,
I tumbled into th' world a gentleman.
She turns her blessèd eye upon me now,   50
And I'll endure all storms before I part with't.
Beatrice. [*Aside*] Again!
    This ominous ill-faced fellow more disturbs me
    Than all my other passions.
De Flores. [*Aside*]   Now't begins again;
    I'll stand this storm of hail though the stones pelt me.   55
Beatrice. Thy business? What's thy business?
De Flores. [*Aside*]   Soft and fair;
    I cannot part so soon now.
Beatrice. [*Aside*]   The villain's fixed—
    [*To De Flores*] Thou standing toad-pool!
De Flores. [*Aside*]   The shower falls amain now.
Beatrice. Who sent thee? What's thy errand? Leave my sight.
De Flores. My lord your father charged me to deliver   60
    A message to you.
Beatrice.   What, another since?
    Do't and be hanged then; let me be rid of thee.
De Flores. True service merits mercy.
Beatrice.   What's thy message?
De Flores. Let beauty settle but in patience,
    You shall hear all.
Beatrice.   A dallying, trifling torment!   65

---

46. *plucked sweets*] enjoyed women's favours.

47. *to his sweet*] in his sweetheart's eyes.

49. *tumbled*] i.e. was born.

56. *Soft and fair*] a proverbial phrase, equivalent to 'calm down and talk politely'.

57. *I . . . now*] You won't get rid of me as easily as you think.

fixed] unmovable, obstinate.

58. *standing toad-pool*] stagnant pool in which repulsive creatures breed (another insulting reference to De Flores' skin disease).

amain] violently, with full force.

61. *another since*] yet another since your previous appearance.

64.] if you, a beautiful woman, will only be patient.

65. *dallying*] time-wasting.

De Flores. Signor Alonzo de Piracquo, lady,
    Sole brother to Tomazo de Piracquo—
Beatrice. Slave, when wilt make an end?
De Flores. [*Aside*]   Too soon I shall.
Beatrice. What all this while of him?
De Flores.   The said Alonzo,
    With the foresaid Tomazo—
Beatrice.   Yet again?   70
De Flores. Is new alighted.
Beatrice.   Vengeance strike the news!
    Thou thing most loathed, what cause was there in this
    To bring thee to my sight?
De Flores.   My lord your father
    Charged me to seek you out.
Beatrice.   Is there no other
    To send his errand by?
De Flores.   It seems 'tis my luck   75
    To be i' th' way still.
Beatrice.   Get thee from me.
De Flores. [*Aside*]   So;
    Why, am not I an ass to devise ways
    Thus to be railed at? I must see her still!
    I shall have a mad qualm within this hour again,
    I know't, and like a common Garden-bull   80
    I do but take breath to be lugged again.
    What this may bode I know not; I'll despair the less,
    Because there's daily precedents of bad faces
    Beloved beyond all reason; these foul chops
    May come into favour one day 'mongst his fellows.   85

---

68. *Slave*] wretch.

71. *strike*] strike down, destroy.

76, 78. *still*] constantly, repeatedly.

78. *railed at*] insulted.

79. *mad qualm*] violent attack (of compulsive desire).

80. *common Garden-bull*] Bull-baiting was carried out at a site in South-wark near the Globe theatre. The first building, known as Paris-Garden, was demolished in 1613 to make way for the Hope theatre, used for both acting and bull- and bear-baiting, and often referred to as the Bear Garden.

81. *lugged*] pulled by the ears (i.e. tormented).

82. *bode*] foretell.

84. *chops*] jaws (but used for the face in general).

Wrangling has proved the mistress of good pastime;
As children cry themselves asleep, I ha' seen
Women have chid themselves abed to men.

                                        Exit DE FLORES.

Beatrice. I never see this fellow but I think
    Of some harm towards me. Danger's in my mind still;   90
    I scarce leave trembling of an hour after.
    The next good mood I find my father in,
    I'll get him quite discarded. Oh, I was
    Lost in this small disturbance, and forgot
    Affliction's fiercer torrent that now comes   95
    To bear down all my comforts.

       Enter VERMANDERO, ALONZO, *and* TOMAZO.

Vermandero.   You're both welcome,
    But an especial one belongs to you, sir,
    To whose most noble name our love presents
    The addition of a son, our son Alonzo.
Alonzo. The treasury of honour cannot bring forth   100
    A title I should more rejoice in, sir.
Vermandero. You have improved it well.—Daughter, prepare;
    The day will steal upon thee suddenly.
Beatrice. [*Aside*] Howe'er, I will be sure to keep the night,
    If it should come so near me.
        [*Beatrice-Joanna and Vermandero talk apart.*]
Tomazo.   Alonzo.
Alonzo.   Brother?   105
Tomazo. In troth I see small welcome in her eye.
Alonzo. Fie, you are too severe a censurer
    Of love in all points; there's no bringing on you.

---

    88. *have . . . men*] who have quarrelled with a man only to end up making love.

    91. *of*] for.

    99. *addition*] title, form of address.

    100. *The treasury of honour*] all the honours and titles given to men.

    102. *improved it well*] made it more noble (by your good behaviour).

    104. *keep the night*] perhaps implying that Beatrice will not allow Alonzo to consummate the marriage.

    107. *censurer*] critic, hostile judge.

    108. *bringing on you*] bringing you to a more reasonable point of view. The quarto has no punctuation after 'you', so the phrase might be linked to the next line: 'persuading you that if lovers . . .'.

If lovers should mark everything a fault,
Affection would be like an ill-set book,   110
Whose faults might prove as big as half the volume.
Beatrice. [*To Vermandero*] That's all I do entreat.
Vermandero.   It is but reasonable.
I'll see what my son says to't.—Son Alonzo,
Here's a motion made but to reprieve
A maidenhead three days longer. The request   115
Is not far out of reason, for indeed
The former time is pinching.
Alonzo.   Though my joys
Be set back so much time as I could wish
They had been forward, yet since she desires it,
The time is set as pleasing as before;   120
I find no gladness wanting.
Vermandero. May I ever meet it in that point still.
You're nobly welcome, sirs.

               Exeunt VERMANDERO *and* BEATRICE-JOANNA.

Tomazo. So; did you mark the dullness of her parting now?
Alonzo. What dullness? Thou art so exceptious still!   125
Tomazo. Why, let it go then. I am but a fool
To mark your harms so heedfully.
Alonzo.   Where's the oversight?
Tomazo. Come, your faith's cozened in her, strongly cozened.
Unsettle your affection with all speed
Wisdom can bring it to; your peace is ruined else.   130
Think what a torment 'tis to marry one
Whose heart is leapt into another's bosom;
If ever pleasure she receive from thee,
It comes not in thy name, or of thy gift.
She lies but with another in thine arms,   135

---

110. *ill-set*] badly set into type.
111. *faults*] misprints.
114. *motion*] proposal.
117. *pinching*] inadequate, causing problems.
122. *meet it in that point*] probably meaning 'arrive at the same conclusion, agree with you'.
124. *dullness*] indifference, lack of warmth.
125. *exceptious*] ready to take exception, make objections.
127. *Where's the oversight?*] What have I failed to notice?
128. *cozened*] cheated.
129. *Unsettle*] remove, detach.
133. *pleasure*] sexual enjoyment.

He the half-father unto all thy children
In the conception; if he get 'em not,
She helps to get 'em for him, and how dangerous
And shameful her restraint may go in time to,
It is not to be thought on without sufferings.   140
Alonzo. You speak as if she loved some other, then.
Tomazo. Do you apprehend so slowly?
Alonzo.   Nay, an that
Be your fear only, I am safe enough.
Preserve your friendship and your counsel, brother,
For times of more distress. I should depart   145
An enemy, a dangerous, deadly one
To any but thyself, that should but think
She knew the meaning of inconstancy,
Much less the use and practice; yet we're friends.
Pray let no more be urged. I can endure   150
Much, till I meet an injury to her;
Then I am not myself. Farewell, sweet brother;
How much we're bound to heaven to depart lovingly.
                                Exit.
Tomazo. Why, here is love's tame madness; thus a man
Quickly steals into his vexation.   *Exit.*   155

[II. ii]

Enter DIAPHANTA *and* ALSEMERO.

Diaphanta. The place is my charge; you have kept your hour,
And the reward of a just meeting bless you.

---

137. *get*] beget.

138.] The quarto reads 'him, in his passions, and', which is hard to explain
and metrically awkward. 'In his passions' might mean 'as though she were
experiencing her lover's passionate desires, not her husband's', but an audience could not easily follow this.

138–40. *how dangerous . . . sufferings*] it is painful to think how dangerously
and shamefully she may behave if too much restraint is imposed on her.

142. *an*] if.

151. *injury*] insult.

153.] i.e. how grateful we should be to heaven that we have parted
amicably.

II.ii.1. *The place . . . charge*] Diaphanta has been responsible for conduct-
ing him to the meeting place through a 'private way' (line 55 below).

I hear my lady coming. Complete gentleman,
I dare not be too busy with my praises;
They're dangerous things to deal with.   *Exit.*
Alsemero.   This goes well.   5
   These women are the ladies' cabinets;
   Things of most precious trust are locked into 'em.

                    Enter BEATRICE-JOANNA.

Beatrice. I have within mine eye all my desires.
   Requests that holy prayers ascend heaven for,
   And brings 'em down to furnish our defects,   10
   Come not more sweet to our necessities
   Than thou unto my wishes.
Alsemero.   We're so like
   In our expressions, lady, that unless I borrow
   The same words I shall never find their equals.
                              [*He kisses her.*]
Beatrice. How happy were this meeting, this embrace,   15
   If it were free from envy! This poor kiss,
   It has an enemy, a hateful one,
   That wishes poison to't. How well were I now
   If there were none such name known as Piracquo,
   Nor no such tie as the command of parents!   20
   I should be but too much blessed.
Alsemero.   One good service
   Would strike off both your fears, and I'll go near it too,

---

4–5.] Beatrice may become suspicious if she overhears Diaphanta praising
Alsemero too enthusiastically.

6. *cabinets*] to which valuable objects (and confidential matters) are en-
trusted.

9–10.] Presumably ''em' are the requests; 'brings' could refer to 'heaven',
though it is more likely to be a singular verb with a plural subject, the
prayers, which ascend to heaven with requests and then bring them back to
us.

10. *furnish our defects*] supply the things we lack.

16. *envy*] ill-will, malice.

16–18. *This poor kiss . . . to't*] The kiss I have just given you has an enemy
(Alonzo) who would like to put poison into it.

22. *strike off*] as fetters are struck off.

go near it] spell it out, be explicit.

Since you are so distressed. Remove the cause,
The command ceases; so there's two fears blown out
With one and the same blast.
Beatrice.   Pray let me find you, sir.   25
    What might that service be so strangely happy?
Alsemero. The honourablest piece 'bout man, valour.
    I'll send a challenge to Piracquo instantly.
Beatrice. How? Call you that extinguishing of fear,
    When 'tis the only way to keep it flaming?   30
    Are not you ventured in the action,
    That's all my joys and comforts? Pray, no more, sir.
    Say you prevailed, you're danger's and not mine then;
    The law would claim you from me, or obscurity
    Be made the grave to bury you alive.   35
    I'm glad these thoughts come forth; oh, keep not one
    Of this condition, sir! Here was a course
    Found to bring sorrow on her way to death;
    The tears would ne'er ha' dried, till dust had choked
        'em.
    Blood-guiltiness becomes a fouler visage—   40
    [*Aside*] And now I think on one; I was to blame
    I ha' marred so good a market with my scorn.
    'T had been done questionless; the ugliest creature

23–4. *Remove . . . ceases*] If Alonzo is removed, your father can no longer order you to marry him. Adapted from the scholastic tag, 'remove the cause and the effect ceases'.

24–5. *so . . . blast*] The metaphor is of blowing out two lights with one breath.

25. *find*] understand.

26. *happy*] having fortunate results.

27. *piece*] quality, attribute.

32. *That's*] you who are.

33. *you're danger's*] you would then belong to danger.

34. *obscurity*] the need to hide away from the law in some obscure place.

36–7. *keep . . . condition*] do not conceal a single thought of this kind.

37–8. *Here . . . death*] This course of action would lead to sorrow and then death.

39. *dust*] the dust of the grave.

40. *becomes*] is appropriate to.

42.] for having been so scornful to someone (De Flores) I could use greatly to my own advantage.

43. *'T had been . . . questionless*] (1) he would certainly have done it; (2) he would have done it without hesitation.

Creation framed for some use, yet to see
I could not mark so much where it should be!   45
Alsemero. Lady—
Beatrice. [*Aside*] Why, men of art make much of poison,
Keep one to expel another; where was my art?
Alsemero. Lady, you hear not me.
Beatrice.   I do especially, sir.
The present times are not so sure of our side
As those hereafter may be; we must use 'em then   50
As thrifty folks their wealth, sparingly now,
Till the time opens.
Alsemero.   You teach wisdom, lady.
Beatrice. [*Calling out*] Within there; Diaphanta!

Enter DIAPHANTA.

Diaphanta.   Do you call, madam?
Beatrice. Perfect your service and conduct this gentleman
The private way you brought him.
Diaphanta.   I shall, madam.   55
Alsemero. My love's as firm as love e'er built upon.
                        Exeunt DIAPHANTA *and* ALSEMERO.

Enter DE FLORES.

De Flores. [*Aside*] I have watched this meeting, and do wonder much
What shall become of t'other; I'm sure both
Cannot be served unless she transgress. Happily

---

44. *for some use*] A current belief was that all objects in nature have some use or function.

45. *mark*] perceive.

it] the use to which De Flores should be put.

46. *art*] learning.

47. *Keep . . . another*] It was a proverbial doctrine that one poison could be used to neutralise another.

where . . . art?] I should have been more skilful.

49. *sure of our side*] clearly working on our behalf.

52. *opens*] becomes more favourable.

54. *Perfect your service*] finish your duty.

58. *t'other*] Alonzo.

59. *Happily*] (1) perhaps; (2) if things go well.

Then I'll put in for one; for if a woman   60
Fly from one point, from him she makes a husband,
She spreads and mounts then like arithmetic—
One, ten, a hundred, a thousand, ten thousand—
Proves in time sutler to an army royal.
Now do I look to be most richly railed at,   65
Yet I must see her.
Beatrice. [*Aside*]   Why, put case I loathed him
As much as youth and beauty hates a sepulchre,
Must I needs show it? Cannot I keep that secret,
And serve my turn upon him?—See, he's here.
[*To him*] De Flores.
De Flores. [*Aside*]   Ha, I shall run mad with joy;   70
She called me fairly by my name De Flores,
And neither 'rogue' nor 'rascal'!
Beatrice.   What ha' you done
To your face alate? You've met with some good
    physician.
You've pruned yourself, methinks; you were not wont
To look so amorously.
De Flores. [*Aside*]   Not I;   75
'Tis the same physnomy, to a hair and pimple,
Which she called scurvy scarce an hour ago.
How is this?
Beatrice.   Come hither; nearer, man!
De Flores. [*Aside*] I'm up to the chin in heaven.
Beatrice. [*Examining his face*]   Turn, let me see.

---

60. *put in for one*] (1) apply for a share (compare IV.iii.37); (2) thrust
myself in as one of her lovers.

61. *Fly . . . point*] De Flores uses the language of falconry; continued in
'mounts', line 62, with sexual suggestion also.

64. *sutler*] camp-follower who sold provisions to soldiers; if a woman,
sometimes a prostitute.

royal] implying 'of a large size', so that she has many customers.

66. *put case*] suppose that.

69. *serve . . . him*] make use of him for my own purposes.

73. *alate*] of late, recently.

74. *pruned*] preened, adorned (used of a bird cleaning and oiling its
feathers).

75. *amorously*] lovely, lovable.

76. *physnomy*] physiognomy, face.

77. *scurvy*] (1) scabby, diseased; (2) contemptible.

Faugh, 'tis but the heat of the liver, I perceive't.   80
I thought it had been worse.
De Flores. [*Aside*]   Her fingers touched me!
She smells all amber.
Beatrice. I'll make a water for you shall cleanse this
Within a fortnight.
De Flores.   With your own hands, lady?
Beatrice. Yes, mine own, sir; in a work of cure   85
I'll trust no other.
De Flores. [*Aside*]   'Tis half an act of pleasure
To hear her talk thus to me.
Beatrice.   When we're used
To a hard face, 'tis not so unpleasing.
It mends still in opinion, hourly mends,
I see it by experience.
De Flores. [*Aside*]   I was blest   90
To light upon this minute; I'll make use on't.
Beatrice. Hardness becomes the visage of a man well;
It argues service, resolution, manhood,
If cause were of employment.
De Flores.   'Twould be soon seen,
If e'er your ladyship had cause to use it.   95
I would but wish the honour of a service
So happy as that mounts to.
Beatrice.   We shall try you—
O my De Flores!
De Flores. [*Aside*]   How's that?
She calls me hers already, *my* De Flores!
[*To Beatrice*] You were about to sigh out somewhat,
madam.   100

---

80. *heat*] inflammation.

liver] traditionally the seat of love and of violent passions generally, so the
remark is truer than Beatrice realises.

81. *worse*] perhaps implying that Beatrice had thought him suffering from
some form of venereal disease.

82. *amber*] ambergris, used to make perfume.

83. *water*] lotion (medicines at the time were often home-made).

shall] that shall.

86–7. *'Tis half . . . me*] To hear Beatrice talking to me in a friendly way
gives me a delight which is halfway to the joy of copulation.

88. *hard*] ugly.

97. *mounts*] amounts (i.e. makes full use of the manly qualities she has just
listed).

Beatrice. No, was I? I forgot,—Oh!
De Flores.   There 'tis again,
    The very fellow on't.
Beatrice.   You are too quick, sir.
De Flores. There's no excuse for't now; I heard it twice,
      madam.
    That sigh would fain have utterance; take pity on't,
    And lend it a free word. 'Las, how it labours   105
    For liberty! I hear the murmur yet
    Beat at your bosom.
Beatrice.   Would creation—
De Flores. Ay, well said, that's it.
Beatrice.   Had formed me man.
De Flores. Nay, that's not it.
Beatrice.   Oh, 'tis the soul of freedom!
    I should not then be forced to marry one   110
    I hate beyond all depths; I should have power
    Then to oppose my loathings, nay, remove 'em
    For ever from my sight.
De Flores.   O blest occasion!—
    Without change to your sex, you have your wishes.
    Claim so much man in me.
Beatrice.   In thee, De Flores?   115
    There's small cause for that.
De Flores.   Put it not from me;
    It's a service that I kneel for to you.   [*He kneels.*]
Beatrice. You are too violent to mean faithfully.
    There's horror in my service, blood and danger;
    Can those be things to sue for?
De Flores.   If you knew   120
    How sweet it were to me to be employed
    In any act of yours, you would say then
    I failed and used not reverence enough
    When I receive the charge on't.
Beatrice. [*Aside*]   This is much, methinks;
    Belike his wants are greedy, and to such   125
    Gold tastes like angels' food. [*To De Flores*] Rise.

---

   113. *occasion*] opportunity.
   124. *This . . . methinks*] Beatrice is surprised by the intensity of De Flores'
reaction, which she attributes to poverty and financial greed.
   126. *angels' food*] manna, food from heaven (Psalm 78.25).

De Flores. I'll have the work first.

Beatrice. [*Aside*]   Possible his need
    Is strong upon him. [*She gives him money.*] There's to
      encourage thee:
    As thou art forward and thy service dangerous,
    Thy reward shall be precious.

De Flores.   That I have thought on;   130
    I have assured myself of that beforehand,
    And know it will be precious; the thought ravishes.

Beatrice. Then take him to thy fury.

De Flores.   I thirst for him.

Beatrice. Alonzo de Piracquo.

De Flores.   His end's upon him;
    He shall be seen no more.   [*He rises.*]

Beatrice.   How lovely now   135
    Dost thou appear to me! Never was man
    Dearlier rewarded.

De Flores.   I do think of that.

Beatrice. Be wondrous careful in the execution.

De Flores. Why, are not both our lives upon the cast?

Beatrice. Then I throw all my fears upon thy service.   140

De Flores. They ne'er shall rise to hurt you.

Beatrice.   When the deed's done,
    I'll furnish thee with all things for thy flight;
    Thou may'st live bravely in another country.

De Flores. Ay, ay, we'll talk of that hereafter.

Beatrice. [*Aside*]   I shall rid myself
    Of two inveterate loathings at one time,   145
    Piracquo, and his dog-face.   *Exit.*

De Flores.   Oh, my blood!

---

127. *Possible*] possibly.

129. *As thou art*] in proportion as, according as.

135. *lovely*] (1) beautiful; (2) lovable.

137. *Dearlier rewarded*] given a richer reward (than he will receive). But 'dear' can mean 'grievous, painful', so there is an unintended irony (cf. 'dearly' at V.i.5 and 105).

139. *cast*] throw of the dice.

143. *bravely*] splendidly.

146. *his dog-face*] either (1) this fellow's ugly face, or (2) an ironical title for De Flores; *his* does not imply that De Flores serves Alonzo.

    blood] sensual desire (compare III.iv.100).

Methinks I feel her in mine arms already,
Her wanton fingers combing out this beard,
And, being pleased, praising this bad face.
Hunger and pleasure, they'll commend sometimes   150
Slovenly dishes, and feed heartily on 'em—
Nay, which is stranger, refuse daintier for 'em.
Some women are odd feeders.—I'm too loud.
Here comes the man goes supperless to bed,
Yet shall not rise tomorrow to his dinner.   155

Enter ALONZO.

Alonzo. De Flores.
De Flores.   My kind, honourable lord?
Alonzo. I am glad I ha' met with thee.
De Flores.   Sir.
Alonzo.   Thou canst show me
    The full strength of the castle?
De Flores.   That I can, sir.
Alonzo. I much desire it.
De Flores.   And if the ways and straits
    Of some of the passages be not too tedious for you, 160
    I will assure you, worth your time and sight, my lord.
Alonzo. Push, that shall be no hindrance.
De Flores.   I'm your servant, then.
    'Tis now near dinner-time; 'gainst your lordship's rising
    I'll have the keys about me.
Alonzo.   Thanks, kind De Flores.
De Flores. [*Aside*] He's safely thrust upon me beyond hopes. 165
                                            Exeunt.

---

149. *being pleased*] having received sexual gratification from me.
150. *commend*] recommend, make acceptable.
151. *Slovenly*] badly prepared.
154-5.] sarcastically implying that Alonzo will be killed before he has a
chance to make love to Beatrice.
159. *straits*] narrow parts.
161. *worth*] it will be worth.
162. *Push*] an exclamation of impatience: Pooh!
163. *'gainst . . . rising*] before your lordship rises from dinner.

Act III

Enter ALONZO *and* DE FLORES.
(*In the act-time De Flores hides a naked rapier.*)

De Flores. Yes, here are all the keys. I was afraid, my lord,
　　I'd wanted for the postern; this is it.
　　I've all, I've all, my lord: this for the sconce.
Alonzo. 'Tis a most spacious and impregnable fort.
De Flores. You'll tell me more, my lord. This descent　　　　5
　　Is somewhat narrow; we shall never pass
　　Well with our weapons, they'll but trouble us.
Alonzo. Thou say'st true.
De Flores.　　　　　　　Pray let me help your lordship.
Alonzo. 'Tis done. Thanks, kind De Flores.
De Flores.　　　　　　　　　　Here are hooks, my lord,
　　To hang such things on purpose.
　　　　　　　　　　　　[*He hangs up the swords.*]
Alonzo.　　　　　　　　　　Lead, I'll follow thee.　　10
　　　　Exeunt at one door and enter at the other.

[III. ii]

De Flores. All this is nothing; you shall see anon

III.i.0.2. act-time] interval between Acts II and III.
naked] without a scabbard.
2. *I'd wanted*] I was without the key.
postern] small back door in a fortification.
3. *sconce*] small fort or earthwork.
5. *You'll . . . more*] You will be even more complimentary later on (but
with an ironic implication, 'you'll soon have something unexpected to respond to').
8–9.] Alonzo takes off his sword-belt, assisted by De Flores.
10.1.] A common stage direction, indicating that a change of scene has
taken place; we are now to imagine that Alonzo and De Flores are some-
where in the underground parts of the castle.

III.ii.1. *anon*] shortly.

A place you little dream on.
Alonzo.   I am glad
 I have this leisure. All your master's house
 Imagine I ha' taken a gondola.
De Flores. All but myself, sir, [*Aside*] which makes up my
  safety.   5
 [*To Alonzo*] My lord, I'll place you at a casement here
 Will show you the full strength of all the castle.
 Look, spend your eye awhile upon that object.
Alonzo. Here's rich variety, De Flores.
De Flores.   Yes, sir.
Alonzo. Goodly munition.
De Flores.   Ay, there's ordnance, sir,   10
 No bastard metal, will ring you a peal like bells
 At great men's funerals. Keep your eye straight, my lord;
 Take special notice of that sconce before you;
 There you may dwell awhile.   [*He takes up the rapier.*]
Alonzo.   I am upon't.
De Flores. And so am I.   [*He stabs him.*]
Alonzo.   De Flores! O De Flores,   15
 Whose malice hast thou put on?
De Flores.   Do you question
 A work of secrecy? I must silence you.   [*He stabs him.*]
Alonzo. Oh, oh, oh!
De Flores.   I must silence you.   [*He stabs him.*]
 So, here's an undertaking well accomplished.
 This vault serves to good use now.—Ha! What's that   20
 Threw sparkles in my eye? Oh, 'tis a diamond

---

 4. *gondola*] small boat (strictly Venetian, but sometimes used in a Spanish context).

 6ff.] Presumably De Flores leads Alonzo to one side of the stage, to a small window which looks on to the underground armoury of the castle (invisible, of course, to the audience). While his back is turned, De Flores picks up the hidden rapier and stabs him.

 10. *munition*] weapons.

 ordnance] large guns.

 11. *bastard*] debased, adulterated.

 will ring you] that will ring. (The colloquial *you* means something like 'for your benefit'.)

 14. *dwell*] a sadistic pun: (1) pause, linger; (2) inhabit (because that is where De Flores will bury his body).

 I am upon't] This phrase is discussed in the Introduction, page 13.

He wears upon his finger. It was well found;
This will approve the work. What, so fast on?
Not part in death? I'll take a speedy course, then;
Finger and all shall off. [*He cuts off the finger.*] So, now I'll
    clear   25
The passages from all suspect or fear.   *Exit with body.*

[III. iii]

Enter ISABELLA *and* LOLLIO.

Isabella. Why, sirrah, whence have you commission
    To fetter the doors against me?
    If you keep me in a cage, pray whistle to me;
    Let me be doing something.
Lollio. You shall be doing, if it please you; I'll whistle to you   5
    if you'll pipe after.
Isabella. Is it your master's pleasure, or your own,
    To keep me in this pinfold?
Lollio. 'Tis for my master's pleasure, lest, being taken in
    another man's corn, you might be pounded in another   10
    place.
Isabella. 'Tis very well, and he'll prove very wise.
Lollio. He says you have company enough in the house, if you
    please to be sociable, of all sorts of people.
Isabella. Of all sorts? Why, here's none but fools and
    madmen.   15
Lollio. Very well; and where will you find any other, if you
    should go abroad? There's my master and I to boot too.
Isabella. Of either sort one, a madman and a fool.

---

23. *approve*] confirm.
26. *suspect*] suspicion.

III.iii.3. *whistle*] whistle a tune, as though to a caged bird.
5–6.] Lollio hints at a possible activity for her ('doing' can mean
'copulating').
I'll whistle . . . after] i.e. I'll try to amuse you if you'll respond to me.
8. *pinfold*] place for confining stray sheep or cattle.
10. *pounded*] impounded, confined as a stray (with obscene implications).
17. *abroad*] out of the house.
18. *Of . . . one*] one of each kind.

Lollio. I would ev'n participate of both then, if I were as you.
    I know you're half mad already; be half foolish too.   20

Isabella. You're a brave saucy rascal! Come on, sir,
    Afford me then the pleasure of your bedlam.
    You were commending once today to me
    Your last-come lunatic, what a proper
    Body there was without brains to guide it,   25
    And what a pitiful delight appeared
    In that defect, as if your wisdom had found
    A mirth in madness. Pray, sir, let me partake,
    If there be such a pleasure.

Lollio. If I do not show you the handsomest, discreetest mad-   30
    man, one that I may call the understanding madman,
    then say I am a fool.

Isabella. Well, a match. I will say so.

Lollio. When you have had a taste of the madman, you shall
    (if you please) see Fools' College, o' th' side. I seldom   35
    lock there; 'tis but shooting a bolt or two, and you are
    amongst 'em.   *Exit.*

Enter [LOLLIO] *presently.*

[*Calling to Franciscus*] Come on, sir; let me see how
handsomely you'll behave yourself now.

Enter FRANCISCUS.

Franciscus. How sweetly she looks! Oh, but there's a wrinkle   40
    in her brow as deep as philosophy. Anacreon, drink to my
    mistress' health, I'll pledge it. Stay, stay, there's a spider

---

19. *participate*] take a share (implying that she should take him as a partner
as well as her husband).

21. *brave saucy*] fine impudent.

24. *last-come*] most recently arrived.
    proper] well-shaped, handsome.

28–9.] Evidently Isabella does not find madness amusing; compare lines
45–6 below.

33. *a match*] agreed!

36. *shooting a bolt*] pulling back a bolt (with a punning allusion to the
proverbial 'a fool's bolt is soon shot', where 'bolt' means 'arrow').

37.1. presently] immediately.

41–3. *Anacreon . . . grape-stone*] The Greek poet Anacreon was supposed
to have choked to death on a grape-stone while drinking a cup of wine.

    in the cup! No, 'tis but a grape-stone; swallow it, fear
    nothing, poet. So, so, lift higher.
Isabella. Alack, alack, 'tis too full of pity   45
    To be laughed at. How fell he mad? Canst thou tell?
Lollio. For love, mistress. He was a pretty poet too, and that
    set him forwards first; the muses then forsook him; he ran
    mad for a chambermaid, yet she was but a dwarf neither.
Franciscus. Hail, bright Titania!   50
    Why stand'st thou idle on these flowery banks?
    Oberon is dancing with his Dryades;
    I'll gather daisies, primrose, violets,
    And bind them in a verse of poesy.
Lollio. Not too near; you see your danger.   55
                        [He shows the whip.]
Franciscus. Oh, hold thy hand, great Diomed;
    Thou feed'st thy horses well; they shall obey thee.
    Get up; Bucephalus kneels.   *[He kneels.]*
Lollio. *[To Isabella]* You see how I awe my flock; a shepherd
    has not his dog at more obedience.   60
Isabella. His conscience is unquiet; sure that was
    The cause of this. A proper gentleman.
Franciscus. Come hither, Esculapius; hide the poison.
                          [He rises.]
Lollio. Well, 'tis hid.

    42–3. *spider in the cup*] Spiders were considered to be poisonous.

    47–8. *that . . . first*] being a poet was his first step towards madness.

    49. *yet . . . neither*] even though she was only a dwarf.

    50–2.] 'Oberon' and 'Titania' are derived presumably from *A Midsummer
Night's Dream*, though 'Oberon' is the traditional name for the king of the
fairies. Franciscus insinuates that Oberon (Alibius) is out enjoying himself
with other women ('dancing with his Dryades'), and suggests that Titania
(Isabella) should solace herself with Franciscus.

    52. *Dryades*] wood-nymphs.

    56. *Diomed*] Diomedes, king of the Bistonians in Thrace, who fed his
horses with human flesh.

    58. *Get up*] mount (as with a horse).

    Bucephalus] the monstrous horse of Alexander the Great, which only he
could ride.

    63. *Esculapius*] the Greek god of healing and medicine. These 'mock-
heroic' descriptions of Lollio are of course sarcastic.

    the poison] the whip; compare line 88.

Franciscus. Didst thou never hear of one Tiresias,   65
    A famous poet?

Lollio. Yes, that kept tame wild geese.

Franciscus. That's he; I am the man.

Lollio. No!

Franciscus. Yes; but make no words on't. I was a man   70
    Seven years ago.

Lollio. A stripling I think you might.

Franciscus. Now I'm a woman, all feminine.

Lollio. I would I might see that.

Franciscus. Juno struck me blind.   75

Lollio. I'll ne'er believe that; for a woman, they say, has an eye
    more than a man.

Franciscus. I say she struck me blind.

Lollio. And Luna made you mad; you have two trades to beg
    with.   80

Franciscus. Luna is now big-bellied, and there's room
    For both of us to ride with Hecate.
    I'll drag thee up into her silver sphere,
    And there we'll kick the dog and beat the bush
    That barks against the witches of the night;   85
    The swift lycanthropi that walks the round,

---

65. *Tiresias*] the famous Theban soothsayer and prophet, who changed into a woman, and then seven years later back into a man. In some versions of his legend he was struck blind by Juno for having revealed that love gave more pleasure to women than to men; see lines 75–8.

66. *poet*] Some editors emend to 'prophet', which is more accurate, but Franciscus is a madman.

67. *wild geese*] This may mean 'prostitutes'.

70. *make . . . on't*] probably meaning 'don't get excited about it'.

72.] Franciscus is young, and seven years ago would have been a boy or youth, not a fully-grown man.

74.] Lollio would like to see visual proof that Franciscus is a woman.

76–7. *an eye . . . man*] probably alluding to the vagina.

79. *Luna*] the moon.

two trades] blindness and madness.

81. *big-bellied*] (1) full; (2) pregnant.

82. *Hecate*] the Greek goddess of witchcraft and magic (but often used to mean simply 'the moon').

84.] The dog and the bush traditionally belong to the Man in the Moon (compare *A Midsummer Night's Dream*, V.i).

86. *lycanthropi*] persons suffering from lycanthropia or wolf-madness, a derangement in which they imagine themselves to be wolves, and behave accordingly.

We'll tear their wolvish skins and save the sheep.

                         [*He tries to seize Lollio.*]

Lollio. Is't come to this? Nay, then my poison comes forth
    again. Mad slave, indeed, abuse your keeper!

Isabella. I prithee hence with him, now he grows dangerous.   90

Franciscus. (*Sings*)

             Sweet love, pity me;

             Give me leave to lie with thee.

Lollio. No, I'll see you wiser first. To your own kennel!

Franciscus. No noise, she sleeps; draw all the curtains round.

    Let no soft sound molest the pretty soul   95

    But love, and love creeps in at a mouse-hole.

Lollio. I would you would get into your hole.

                          Exit FRANCISCUS.

Now, mistress, I will bring you another sort; you shall be
    fooled another while. [*Calling*] Tony, come hither, Tony;
    look who's yonder, Tony.   100

                 Enter ANTONIO.

Antonio. Cousin, is it not my aunt?

Lollio. Yes, 'tis one of 'em, Tony.

Antonio. He, he! How do you, uncle?

Lollio. Fear him not, mistress, 'tis a gentle nidget; you may
    play with him, as safely with him as with his bauble.   105

Isabella. How long hast thou been a fool?

Antonio. Ever since I came hither, cousin.

Isabella. Cousin? I'm none of thy cousins, fool.

Lollio. Oh, mistress, fools have always so much wit as to claim
    their kindred.   110

---

    89. *abuse*] to behave violently towards.

    94. *she*] the woman to whom his song was addressed.

    99. *fooled*] (1) entertained by a fool; (2) made a fool of.

    101. *aunt*] sometimes used to mean prostitute or bawd.

    104. *nidget*] idiot.

    105. *bauble*] baton or stick carried by fools (with obscene implications).

    106–7.] Isabella may be suspicious about Antonio; if so, his reply will not
reassure her.

    107. *cousin*] Often in Elizabethan drama an unfaithful woman and her
lover gain access to each other by pretending to be cousins. This may help to
account for Isabella's indignant repudiation of the relationship.

Madman. (*Within*) Bounce, bounce, he falls, he falls!

Isabella. Hark you, your scholars in the upper room
    Are out of order.

Lollio. [*Calling*] Must I come amongst you there?—Keep you
    the fool, mistress; I'll go up and play left-handed Orlando   115
    amongst the madmen.   *Exit.*

Isabella. Well, sir.   [*Antonio drops his mad guise.*]

Antonio. 'Tis opportuneful now, sweet lady! Nay,
    Cast no amazing eye upon this change.

Isabella. Ha!   120

Antonio. This shape of folly shrouds your dearest love,
    The truest servant to your powerful beauties,
    Whose magic had this force thus to transform me.

Isabella. You are a fine fool indeed.

Antonio.   Oh, 'tis not strange.
    Love has an intellect that runs through all   125
    The scrutinous sciences, and like
    A cunning poet catches a quantity
    Of every knowledge, yet brings all home
    Into one mystery, into one secret
    That he proceeds in.

Isabella.   You're a parlous fool.   130

Antonio. No danger in me; I bring nought but love
    And his soft-wounding shafts to strike you with.
    Try but one arrow; if it hurt you,
    I'll stand you twenty back in recompense.

                                [*He kisses her.*]

---

111. *Bounce*] bang, the noise of a gun.

115. *left-handed Orlando*] The reference is presumably to the hero of
Ariosto's *Orlando Furioso*. 'Left-handed' can mean 'clumsy, awkward', and
may imply that Lollio doubts his ability to impose order among the madmen.

118. *opportuneful*] providing an opportunity.

119. *amazing*] amazed.

change] altered behaviour.

121. *shrouds*] conceals.

126. *scrutinous sciences*] branches of learning which examine things closely.

127. *cunning*] skilful.

129. *mystery*] skilled practice of an art, known only to the initiated.

130. *parlous*] mischievous, dangerous.

131. *love*] here a masculine figure (Cupid).

134. *stand*] give.

Isabella. A forward fool too!

Antonio.   This was love's teaching: 135
  A thousand ways he fashioned out my way,
  And this I found the safest and the nearest
  To tread the Galaxia to my star.

Isabella. Profound, withal! Certain, you dreamed of this;
  Love never taught it waking.

Antonio.   Take no acquaintance   140
  Of these outward follies; there is within
  A gentleman that loves you.

Isabella.   When I see him,
  I'll speak with him; so in the meantime keep
  Your habit, it becomes you well enough.
  As you are a gentleman, I'll not discover you;   145
  That's all the favour that you must expect.
  When you are weary, you may leave the school,
  For all this while you have but played the fool.

Enter LOLLIO.

Antonio. And must again.—He, he! I thank you, cousin;
  I'll be your valentine tomorrow morning.   150

Lollio. How do you like the fool, mistress?

Isabella. Passing well, sir.

Lollio. Is he not witty, pretty well for a fool?

Isabella. If he hold on as he begins, he is like
  To come to something.   155

Lollio. Ay, thank a good tutor. You may put him to't; he

---

135. *forward*] impudent.

136.] He suggested a thousand ways for me to approach you.

138. *Galaxia*] Milky Way.

139. *Profound, withal*] You are ingenious, as well! (She has already described him as 'parlous' and 'forward'.)

140–1. *Take . . . follies*] Ignore my outward appearance.

145. *discover*] reveal.

148. *played the fool*] (1) acted the role of a fool; (2) made a fool of yourself; (3) wasted your time.

149. *And . . . again*] I must behave as a fool again.

150.] Perhaps echoing Ophelia's song in *Hamlet*, IV.v.48ff. ('Tomorrow is Saint Valentine's day, / All in the morning betime . . .'), or a lost popular ballad from which the song perhaps derives.

152. *Passing*] exceedingly.

begins to answer pretty hard questions.—Tony, how
many is five times six?

Antonio. Five times six is six times five.

Lollio. What arithmetician could have answered better?—   160
How many is one hundred and seven?

Antonio. One hundred and seven is seven hundred and one,
cousin.

Lollio. [*To Isabella*] This is no wit to speak on. Will you be rid
of the fool now?   165

Isabella. By no means; let him stay a little.

Madman. (*Within*) Catch there, catch the last couple in hell!

Lollio. Again? Must I come amongst you? Would my master
were come home! I am not able to govern both these
wards together.   *Exit.*   170

Antonio. Why should a minute of love's hour be lost?

Isabella. Fie, out again! I had rather you kept
Your other posture; you become not your tongue
When you speak from your clothes.

Antonio.   How can he freeze,
Lives near so sweet a warmth? Shall I alone   175
Walk through the orchard of the Hesperides,
And cowardly not dare to pull an apple?
This with the red cheeks I must venture for.
                        [*He tries to kiss her.*]

---

164. *This . . . on*] Lollio seems to have changed his mind and decided that
Antonio is not really intelligent.

167.] An allusion to 'barley-break', a country game played by three mixed
couples. One couple, who occupied a central area known as 'hell', held hands
and were not allowed to separate; they tried to catch the others as they ran
through the central space in order to change partners. Those who were
caught had to replace the original couple in hell. See V.iii.162–3.

169–70. *both these wards*] the fools' and the madmen's wards.

172. *out*] i.e. not playing your role as a fool.

173–4. *you become . . . clothes*] i.e. the clothes you are wearing do not suit
you when you speak seriously.

174–5. *How . . . warmth?*] How can any man fail to be stimulated by your
presence?

175. *Lives*] who lives.

176. *Hesperides*] In the garden of the Hesperides there grew a tree with
golden apples; one of the labours of Hercules was to kill the dragon guarding
the tree and carry off the apples.

Enter LOLLIO *above.*

Isabella. Take heed, there's giants keep 'em.
Lollio. [*Aside*] How now, fool, are you good at that? Have you   180
     read Lipsius? He's past *Ars Amandi*; I believe I must put
     harder questions to him, I perceive that.
Isabella. You are bold without fear too.
Antonio.   What should I fear,
     Having all joys about me? Do you smile,
     And love shall play the wanton on your lip,   185
     Meet and retire, retire and meet again.
     Look you but cheerfully, and in your eyes
     I shall behold mine own deformity
     And dress myself up fairer. I know this shape
     Becomes me not, but in those bright mirrors   190
     I shall array me handsomely.
Lollio. Cuckoo, cuckoo!   *Exit.*

     [*Enter*] Madmen *above, some as birds, others as beasts.*

Antonio. What are these?
Isabella.   Of fear enough to part us;
     Yet are they but our schools of lunatics,
     That act their fantasies in any shapes   195
     Suiting their present thoughts. If sad, they cry;
     If mirth be their conceit, they laugh again.

---

179. *giants*] a sarcastic reference to Lollio and Isabella's husband, who are
trying to guard her like the dragon of the Hesperides.

181. *Lipsius*] Justus Lipsius (1547–1606) was a famous scholar and jurist.
The name is brought in for the sake of a pun on 'lips'.

Ars Amandi] Ovid's *Ars Amandi* (*The Art of Loving*) is a witty handbook on
the art of seduction. Lollio's remark means (1) that Antonio has mastered the
treatise and needs to move on to more difficult textbooks; (2) that he is
showing himself to be a skilful seducer.

184. *Do you smile*] Do but smile.

190. *mirrors*] Isabella's eyes.

192. *Cuckoo, cuckoo!*] implying that Alibius is about to be cuckolded.

192.1] The madmen make bird and beast noises, but lines 198–9 do not
necessarily imply that they dress in bird and beast costumes, as some scholars
argue. This is their usual behaviour, not part of the wedding entertainment
described later, which Isabella does not know about.

193. *Of fear*] fearful, frightening.

197. *conceit*] fanciful notion.

Sometimes they imitate the beasts and birds,
Singing, or howling, braying, barking—all
As their wild fancies prompt 'em.

                        [*Exeunt* Madmen *above.*]

                Enter LOLLIO.

Antonio.   These are no fears.   200
Isabella. But here's a large one, my man.
Antonio. Ha, he! That's fine sport indeed, cousin.
Lollio. I would my master were come home. 'Tis too much for
   one shepherd to govern two of these flocks; nor can I
   believe that one churchman can instruct two benefices at   205
   once; there will be some incurable mad of the one side,
   and very fools on the other.—Come, Tony.
Antonio. Prithee, cousin, let me stay here still.
Lollio. No, you must to your book now you have played
   sufficiently.   210
Isabella. Your fool is grown wondrous witty.
Lollio. Well, I'll say nothing; but I do not think but he will put
   you down one of these days.

                   Exeunt LOLLIO *and* ANTONIO.
Isabella. Here the restrainèd current might make breach,
   Spite of the watchful bankers. Would a woman stray,   215
   She need not gad abroad to seek her sin;
   It would be brought home one ways or other.
   The needle's point will to the fixèd north;
   Such drawing arctics women's beauties are.

201.] Here comes a real threat, my servant Lollio.

202.] Antonio again reverts to his role as a fool.

204–6. *nor . . . once*] a jibe at the practice of pluralism, by which a clergy-man held two or more benefices simultaneously.

206. *of*] on.

212–13. *put you down*] defeat you in an argument (with an obscene implication).

215. *bankers*] labourers who make banks of earth, dykes, etc.

218. *needle's point*] point of a compass (but with phallic implications).
will] will move.

219. *arctics*] North poles.

Enter LOLLIO.

Lollio. How dost thou, sweet rogue?   220
Isabella. How now?
Lollio. Come, there are degrees; one fool may be better than
    another.
Isabella. What's the matter?
Lollio. Nay, if thou giv'st thy mind to fool's flesh, have at thee!   225
                         [*He tries to kiss her.*]
Isabella. You bold slave, you!
Lollio. I could follow now as t'other fool did:
    'What should I fear,
    Having all joys about me? Do you but smile,
    And love shall play the wanton on your lip,   230
    Meet and retire, retire and meet again.
    Look you but cheerfully, and in your eyes
    I shall behold my own deformity
    And dress myself up fairer. I know this shape
    Becomes me not—' And so as it follows; but is not this   235
    the more foolish way? Come, sweet rogue; kiss me, my
    little Lacedemonian. Let me feel how thy pulses beat;
    thou hast a thing about thee would do a man pleasure, I'll
    lay my hand on't.
Isabella. Sirrah, no more! I see you have discovered   240
    This love's knight-errant, who hath made adventure
    For purchase of my love. Be silent, mute,
    Mute as a statue, or his injunction
    For me enjoying shall be to cut thy throat.

---

225. *have at thee!*] here I come!

227.] I could continue in the language of Antonio (Lollio evidently
overheard Antonio's speech at lines 183–91 above).

236. *the more foolish way*] a silly way to woo you (Lollio prefers a more
direct approach).

237. *Lacedemonian*] (1) someone laconic in speech; (2) slang for
'prostitute'.

238. *thing*] a euphemism for the female genitals.

238–9. *I'll . . . on't*] equivalent to modern 'I'll bet', with a play of words on
lay as meaning 'place'.

241. *love's knight-errant*] wandering knight inspired by love (i.e. Antonio).

242. *For purchase*] to obtain as a prize or reward.

243–4. *his injunction . . . enjoying*] what he will have to do in order to gain
my love.

I'll do it, though for no other purpose,   245
    And be sure he'll not refuse it.
Lollio. My share, that's all; I'll have my fool's part with you.
Isabella. No more! Your master.

Enter ALIBIUS.

Alibius.   Sweet, how dost thou?
Isabella. Your bounden servant, sir.
Alibius.   Fie, fie, sweetheart,
    No more of that.
Isabella.   You were best lock me up.   250
Alibius. In my arms and bosom, my sweet Isabella,
    I'll lock thee up most nearly.—Lollio,
    We have employment, we have task in hand;
    At noble Vermandero's, our castle-captain,
    There is a nuptial to be solemnised   255
    (Beatrice-Joanna, his fair daughter, bride),
    For which the gentleman hath bespoke our pains:
    A mixture of our madmen and our fools,
    To finish, as it were, and make the fag
    Of all the revels, the third night from the first.   260
    Only an unexpected passage over,
    To make a frightful pleasure, that is all,
    But not the all I aim at; could we so act it,
    To teach it in a wild distracted measure,
    Though out of form and figure, breaking time's head,   265

245.] I'll make the arrangement merely for the sake of getting rid of you.

249. *bounden*] a play on words similar to 'bound' at I.i.220; Isabella resents the restraints laid upon her by Alibius.

250. *You were best*] you had better.

257. *bespoke our pains*] commissioned our best efforts.

259. *fag*] fag-end, last bit.

260.] The wedding celebrations will last for three days.

261ff.] The entertainment is less ambitious than a formal masque: the madmen and fools will rush in suddenly and dance, but in a grotesque way that will give a 'frightful pleasure' to the audience.

over] into and out of the hall in which the ceremonies are taking place.

264. *teach*] show, present.

265. *breaking time's head*] not keeping time or following a strict rhythmical pattern.

It were no matter, 'twould be healed again
In one age or other, if not in this.
This, this, Lollio, there's a good reward begun,
And will beget a bounty, be it known.

Lollio. This is easy, sir, I'll warrant you. You have about you   270
fools and madmen that can dance very well, and 'tis no
wonder your best dancers are not the wisest men; the
reason is, with often jumping they jolt their brains down
into their feet, that their wits lie more in their heels than
in their heads.   275

Alibius. Honest Lollio, thou giv'st me a good reason,
And a comfort in it.

Isabella.   You've a fine trade on't;
Madmen and fools are a staple commodity.

Alibius. Oh, wife, we must eat, wear clothes, and live.
Just at the lawyer's haven we arrive;   280
By madmen and by fools we both do thrive.   *Exeunt.*

[III. iv]

Enter VERMANDERO, ALSEMERO, JASPERINO,
and BEATRICE-JOANNA.

Vermandero. [*To Alsemero*] Valencia speaks so nobly of you,
sir,
I wish I had a daughter now for you.

Alsemero. The fellow of this creature were a partner
For a king's love.

Vermandero.   I had her fellow once, sir,
But heaven has married her to joys eternal;   5

266.] *healed* seems to refer back to *breaking* (i.e. wounding) *time's head*;
with experience they will be able to perform better in future.

269.] let it be known that a good performance will be generously
rewarded.

277. *on't*] in it.

278.] a sarcastic observation that fools and madmen are now essential
items in trade and commerce.

280-1.] implying that those who go to law are fools and madmen.

III.iv.3-4. *The fellow . . . love*] Another creature perfectly like Beatrice
(and, implicitly, she herself) would be fit to be a queen.

4. *fellow*] Beatrice's mother, now dead.

'Twere sin to wish her in this vale again.
Come, sir, your friend and you shall see the pleasures
Which my health chiefly joys in.
Alsemero. I hear the beauty of this seat largely.
Vermandero. It falls much short of that.

Exeunt. Manet BEATRICE-JOANNA.

Beatrice.   So, here's one step   10
Into my father's favour; time will fix him.
I have got him now the liberty of the house;
So wisdom by degrees works out her freedom.
And if that eye be darkened that offends me
(I wait but that eclipse), this gentleman   15
Shall soon shine glorious in my father's liking,
Through the refulgent virtue of my love.

Enter DE FLORES.

De Flores. [*Aside*] My thoughts are at a banquet for the deed.
I feel no weight in't; 'tis but light and cheap
For the sweet recompense that I set down for't.   20
Beatrice. De Flores.
De Flores.   Lady?
Beatrice.   Thy looks promise cheerfully.
De Flores. All things are answerable—time, circumstance,
Your wishes, and my service.
Beatrice.   Is it done then?
De Flores. Piracquo is no more.

---

6. *vale*] vale of tears, human life seen as painful.

8.] which are the chief solace of what health I am able to enjoy.

9. *seat*] location and surroundings of Vermandero's castle (compare *Macbeth*, I.vi.1).

largely] widely reported.

10. S.D. Manet] remains on stage.

14.] An echo of the New Testament: 'And if thine eye offend thee . . .' (e.g. Matthew, 18.9). She is thinking of Alonzo.

17. *refulgent*] bright, radiant.

18. *at . . . deed*] gloating over the reward I expect for having murdered Alonzo.

20. *set down*] specified.

22. *answerable*] fitting, convenient.

Beatrice. [*Weeping*] My joys start at mine eyes; our sweet'st
    delights   25
    Are evermore born weeping.
De Flores.   I've a token for you.
Beatrice. For me?
De Flores.   But it was sent somewhat unwillingly.
    I could not get the ring without the finger.
                      [*He offers her the finger.*]
Beatrice. Bless me! What hast thou done?
De Flores.   Why, is that more
    Than killing the whole man? I cut his heart-strings.   30
    A greedy hand thrust in a dish at court
    In a mistake hath had as much as this.
Beatrice. 'Tis the first token my father made me send him.
De Flores. And I made him send it back again
    For his last token; I was loath to leave it,   35
    And I'm sure dead men have no use of jewels.
    He was as loath to part with't, for it stuck
    As if the flesh and it were both one substance.
Beatrice. At the stag's fall the keeper has his fees.
    'Tis soon applied; all dead men's fees are yours, sir.   40
    I pray, bury the finger, but the stone
    You may make use on shortly; the true value,
    Take't of my truth, is near three hundred ducats.
De Flores. 'Twill hardly buy a capcase for one's conscience,
    though,
    To keep it from the worm, as fine as 'tis.   45

25–6.] Weeping as a sign of joy is frequent in Middleton's plays, but here
the idea has a pungent irony not found elsewhere.

26. *token*] (1) proof of my action (2) love token (see lines 33 and 35).

30. *heart-strings*] tendons or nerves enabling the heart to function.

31–2.] The courtier has pushed his hand into the dish to take food and has
had a finger cut off by someone else's knife.

39.] At the killing of a stag the gamekeeper was entitled to certain parts of
the animal as his fees.

40. *'Tis soon applied*] The relevance of the preceding line is immediately
obvious.

43. *Take't . . . truth*] believe what I say to be true.
ducats] valuable gold coins.

44. *capcase*] small travelling case, wallet.

45. *worm*] pangs of guilt or remorse.

Well, being my fees I'll take it;
Great men have taught me that, or else my merit
Would scorn the way on't.
Beatrice.   It might justly, sir.
Why, thou mistak'st, De Flores, 'tis not given
In state of recompense.
De Flores.   No, I hope so, lady.   50
You should soon witness my contempt to't then!
Beatrice. Prithee, thou look'st as if thou wert offended.
De Flores. That were strange, lady; 'tis not possible
My service should draw such a cause from you.
Offended? Could you think so? That were much   55
For one of my performance, and so warm
Yet in my service.
Beatrice. 'Twere misery in me to give you cause, sir.
De Flores. I know so much, it were so—misery
In her most sharp condition.
Beatrice.   'Tis resolved, then.   60
                    [*She offers him money.*]
Look you, sir, here's three thousand golden florins;
I have not meanly thought upon thy merit.
De Flores. What, salary? Now you move me.
Beatrice.   How, De Flores?
De Flores. Do you place me in the rank of verminous fellows,
To destroy things for wages? Offer gold?   65
The life blood of man! Is anything
Valued too precious for my recompense?

---

47. *Great . . . that*] perhaps sarcastically implying that great men, even though they are wealthy and he is not, never refuse to accept money.

my merit] my sense of true deserving.

48. *the way on't*] this way of rewarding me.

54. *cause*] accusation.

58–9. *misery*] Beatrice means 'a miserable thing (an act of ingratitude)'; De Flores' reply gives it a sharper and more threatening sense ('painful suffering').

61. *florins*] gold coins. Three thousand coins would be bulky and heavy; perhaps she offers him a promissory note.

62. *meanly*] ungenerously.

63. *move*] provoke to anger.

Beatrice. I understand thee not.
De Flores.   I could ha' hired
    A journeyman in murder at this rate,
    And mine own conscience might have slept at ease,   70
    And have had the work brought home.
Beatrice. [*Aside*]   I'm in a labyrinth;
    What will content him? I would fain be rid of him.
    [*To De Flores*] I'll double the sum sir.
De Flores.   You take a course
    To double my vexation, that's the good you do.
Beatrice. [*Aside*] Bless me! I am now in worse plight than I
        was;   75
    I know not what will please him. [*To De Flores*] For my
        fear's sake,
    I prithee make away with all speed possible.
    And if thou be'st so modest not to name
    The sum that will content thee, paper blushes not;
    Send thy demand in writing, it shall follow thee,   80
    But prithee take thy flight.
De Flores.   You must fly too then.
Beatrice. I?
De Flores. I'll not stir a foot else.
Beatrice.   What's your meaning?
De Flores. Why, are not you as guilty, in (I'm sure)
    As deep as I? And we should stick together.
    Come, your fears counsel you but ill; my absence   85
    Would draw suspect upon you instantly.
    There were no rescue for you.
Beatrice. [*Aside*]   He speaks home.

68–9. *I . . . rate*] i.e. For this amount of money I could have hired a
professional murderer.

70.] The quarto ends at 'have', and 'slept at ease' is an editorial addition.

71.] *Home* is ambiguous, and the line could mean either (1) 'and have got
someone else to carry out the job in a forcible manner' (see line 87 below),
or (2) 'and have waited quietly at home for someone else to do the job and
report back to me'.

74. *that's the good*] that's all the good.

77. *make away*] get away, flee.

86. *suspect*] suspicion.

87. *home*] forcibly.

De Flores. Nor is it fit we two, engaged so jointly, —

  Should part and live asunder.   [*He tries to kiss her.*]

Beatrice.   How now, sir?

  This shows not well.

De Flores.   What makes your lip so strange?   90

  This must not be betwixt us.

Beatrice. [*Aside*]   The man talks wildly.

De Flores. Come, kiss me with a zeal now.

Beatrice. [*Aside*]   Heaven, I doubt him!

De Flores. I will not stand so long to beg 'em shortly.

Beatrice. Take heed, De Flores, of forgetfulness;

  'Twill soon betray us.

De Flores.   Take you heed first;   95

  Faith, you're grown much forgetful; you're to blame in't.

Beatrice. [*Aside*] He's bold, and I am blamed for't!

De Flores.   I have eased you

  Of your trouble; think on't. I'm in pain,

  And must be eased of you; 'tis a charity.

  Justice invites your blood to understand me.   100

Beatrice. I dare not.

De Flores.   Quickly!

Beatrice.   Oh, I never shall!

  Speak it yet further off that I may lose

  What has been spoken, and no sound remain on't.

  I would not hear so much offence again

  For such another deed.

De Flores.   Soft, lady, soft;   105

  The last is not yet paid for! Oh, this act

  Has put me into spirit; I was as greedy on't

---

88. *engaged so jointly*] collaborating so closely.

90. *strange*] cold, unfriendly.

92. *doubt*] mistrust, suspect, fear.

93.] I will not stand here begging for your favours much longer.

94. *forgetfulness*] a favourite word of Middleton's; here meaning 'forgetting that you are a servant and should treat me with respect', but capable of a wider significance (forgetting the restraints of morality).

96. *forgetful*] ungrateful, failing to remember now much I have done.

100. *blood*] here meaning 'sexuality'.

102. *lose*] be unable to hear, forget.

104. *offence*] offensive speech.

As the parched earth of moisture, when the clouds weep.
Did you not mark, I wrought myself into't,
Nay, sued and kneeled for't; why was all that pains took? 110
You see I have thrown contempt upon your gold—
Not that I want it not, for I do piteously;
In order I will come unto't and make use on't,
But 'twas not held so precious to begin with.
For I place wealth after the heels of pleasure,   115
And were I not resolved in my belief
That thy virginity were perfect in thee,
I should but take my recompense with grudging,
As if I had but half my hopes I agreed for.
Beatrice. Why, 'tis impossible thou canst be so wicked,   120
Or shelter such a cunning cruelty,
To make his death the murderer of my honour!
Thy language is so bold and vicious,
I cannot see which way I can forgive it
With any modesty.
De Flores.   Push, you forget yourself!   125
A woman dipped in blood, and talk of modesty?
Beatrice. Oh, misery of sin! Would I had been bound
Perpetually unto my living hate
In that Piracquo than to hear these words.
Think but upon the distance that creation   130
Set 'twixt thy blood and mine, and keep thee there.
De Flores. Look but into your conscience, read me there;
'Tis a true book; you'll find me there your equal.
Push, fly not to your birth, but settle you
In what the act has made you; you're no more now.   135
You must forget your parentage to me:
You're the deed's creature; by that name

---

109. *wrought myself into't*] arranged for myself to do the deed.
113. *In order*] in due time.
115.] Money is secondary to (sexual) pleasure.
116. *resolved*] certain, convinced.
122. *his*] Alonzo's.
130. *creation*] the social order as created by God.
131. *blood*] social rank.
136. *to*] in favour of.
137. *the deed's creature*] (1) created or transformed by the deed; (2) enslaved to it.

> You lost your first condition, and I challenge you,
> As peace and innocency has turned you out,
> And made you one with me.
> Beatrice.   With thee, foul villain?   140
> De Flores. Yes, my fair murd'ress; do you urge me?
>> Though thou writ'st maid, thou whore in thy affection!
>> 'Twas changed from thy first love, and that's a kind
>> Of whoredom in thy heart; and he's changed now,
>> To bring thy second on, thy Alsemero,   145
>> Whom (by all sweets that ever darkness tasted)
>> If I enjoy thee not, thou ne'er enjoy'st.
>> I'll blast the hopes and joys of marriage.
>> I'll confess all; my life I rate at nothing.
> Beatrice. De Flores!   150
> De Flores. I shall rest from all lovers' plagues then.
>> I live in pain now; that shooting eye
>> Will burn my heart to cinders.
> Beatrice.   Oh, sir, hear me.
> De Flores. She that in life and love refuses me,
>> In death and shame my partner she shall be.   155
> Beatrice. Stay, hear me once for all! [She kneels.] I make thee
>> master
>> Of all the wealth I have in gold and jewels;
>> Let me go poor unto my bed with honour,
>> And I am rich in all things.
> De Flores.   Let this silence thee:
>> The wealth of all Valencia shall not buy   160
>> My pleasure from me.
>> Can you weep fate from its determined purpose?

---

138. *challenge*] claim.

139. *turned you out*] rejected you.

141. *urge*] provoke, incite.

142. *writ'st maid*] would call yourself a virgin.

143. *first love*] Alonzo (this suggests that Beatrice thought herself genuinely in love with Alonzo when she was betrothed to him, and was not merely obeying her father).

144. *changed*] a sarcastic allusion to Alonzo's death.

151.] i.e. After confession I shall be executed and then will be freed from the torments that all lovers suffer.

152. *shooting*] sending out provocative glances.

So soon may you weep me.
Beatrice.   Vengeance begins;
   Murder I see is followed by more sins.
   Was my creation in the womb so cursed   165
   It must engender with a viper first?
De Flores. Come, rise, and shroud your blushes in my bosom.
                                        [*He raises her.*]
   Silence is one of pleasure's best receipts;
   Thy peace is wrought for ever in this yielding.
   'Las, how the turtle pants! Thou'lt love anon   170
   What thou so fear'st and faint'st to venture on.
                                        Exeunt.

   165–6.] i.e. When I was created in my mother's womb, was a curse laid
upon me that I must engender with an unnatural being, a viper, before I
could do so with a normal man?
   167. *shroud*] hide.
   168. *receipts*] recipes, means towards.
   170. *turtle*] turtle-dove.

Act IV

[IV. i]

[*Dumb Show*]

Enter Gentlemen, VERMANDERO *meeting them with action of wonder-
ment at the flight of Piracquo. Enter* ALSEMERO, *with* JASPERINO, *and*
Gallants; *Vermandero points to him, the Gentlemen seeming to ap-
plaud the choice;* [*Exeunt in procession*] ALSEMERO, JASPERINO, *and*
Gentlemen; BEATRICE-JOANNA *the bride following in great state,
accompanied with* DIAPHANTA, ISABELLA *and other* Gentlewomen;
DE FLORES *after all, smiling at the accident.* ALONZO'S GHOST
*appears to De Flores in the midst of his smile, startles him, showing him
the hand whose finger he had cut off. They pass over in great solemnity.*

Enter BEATRICE-JOANNA.

Beatrice. This fellow has undone me endlessly;
 Never was bride so fearfully distressed.
 The more I think upon th'ensuing night,
 And whom I am to cope with in embraces—
 One that's ennobled both in blood and mind,   5
 So clear in understanding (that's my plague now),
 Before whose judgement will my fault appear
 Like malefactors' crimes before tribunals,
 There is no hiding on't—the more I dive
 Into my own distress. How a wise man   10

IV.i.0.2. flight] Vermandero assumes that Alonzo has jilted Beatrice (see
IV.ii.24–32).

0.7. accident] way events have occurred.

0.9. pass over] cross the stage and exit.

solemnity] ceremoniousness.

1. *undone me endlessly*] caused me infinite trouble (but also implying,
probably unconsciously, 'damned me eternally').

4. *whom*] i.e. Alsemero.

6. *that's . . . now*] Alsemero's intelligence is now potentially dangerous.

9–10. *the more . . . distress*] the deeper I plunge into misery (follows from
'The more I think . . . embraces' in lines 3–4).

Stands for a great calamity! There's no venturing
Into his bed, what course soe'er I light upon,
Without my shame, which may grow up to danger.
He cannot but in justice strangle me
As I lie by him, as a cheater use me.   15
'Tis a precious craft to play with a false die
Before a cunning gamester. Here's his closet,
The key left in't, and he abroad i' th' park.
Sure 'twas forgot; I'll be so bold as look in't.
                              [*She opens the closet.*]
Bless me! A right physician's closet 'tis,   20
Set round with vials, every one her mark too.
Sure he does practise physic for his own use,
Which may be safely called your great man's wisdom.
What manuscript lies here? 'The Book of Experiment,
Called Secrets in Nature'; so 'tis, 'tis so.   25
'How to know whether a woman be with child or no.'
I hope I am not yet; if he should try, though!
Let me see, folio forty-five. Here 'tis;
The leaf tucked down upon't, the place suspicious.
'If you would know whether a woman be with child or   30

---

11. *Stands for*] represents (because he is harder to deceive).
13. *grow . . . danger*] increase to the point of being dangerous.
15. *as . . . me*] treat me as someone who cheats at gambling.
16. *precious*] subtle, risky.
die] singular of 'dice'.
17. *closet*] small private room, study.
20. *right*] true.
21. *vials*] small bottles.
her mark] with a mark or letter identifying the contents.
23.] because it protects him against poison.
25. *Secrets in Nature*] *De Arcanis Naturae* is the title of a book by Antonius Mizaldus (1520–78), a French scholar and compiler of various works of science and pseudo-science (see lines 45–6). There are no tests in it resembling those quoted by Beatrice, but virginity and pregnancy tests occur in other writings by him and in numerous other authors. Lines 24 and 45–6 suggest that Beatrice is quoting from a manuscript miscellany compiled by Alsemero himself.
26.] Beatrice is reading through the list of contents.

not, give her two spoonfuls of the white water in glass
C—'
Where's that glass C? Oh, yonder, I see't now—
'and if she be with child, she sleeps full twelve hours after;
if not, not.'   35
None of that water comes into my belly.
I'll know you from a hundred; I could break you now,
Or turn you into milk, and so beguile
The master of the mystery, but I'll look to you.
Ha! That which is next is ten times worse.   40
'How to know whether a woman be a maid or not';
If that should be applied, what would become of me?
Belike he has a strong faith of my purity,
That never yet made proof; but this he calls
'A merry sleight, but true experiment, the author   45
Antonius Mizaldus. Give the party you suspect the
quantity of a spoonful of the water in the glass M, which
upon her that is a maid makes three several effects: 'twill
make her incontinently gape, then fall into a sudden
sneezing, last into a violent laughing; else dull, heavy,   50
and lumpish.'
Where had I been?
I fear it; yet 'tis seven hours to bedtime.

Enter DIAPHANTA.

Diaphanta. Cuds, madam, are you here?
Beatrice. [*Aside*]   Seeing that wench now,

31, 36. *water*] liquid.
39. *mystery*] secret (i.e. the formula used in the pregnancy test).
look to] keep watch on.
42. *applied*] tried on me.
43. *Belike*] probably.
44. *That*] who.
45. *sleight*] trick, device.
48. *several*] separate.
49. *incontinently gape*] immediately yawn.
50. *else*] otherwise.
52.] i.e. Where would I have been if I had not discovered this?
54. *Cuds*] a corruption of 'God's', used as a mild oath.

A trick comes in my mind; 'tis a nice piece   55
Gold cannot purchase. [*To Diaphanta*] I come hither,
    wench,
To look my lord.
Diaphanta. [*Aside*] Would I had such a cause to look him too!
    [*To Beatrice*] Why, he's i' th' park, madam.
Beatrice. There let him be.
Diaphanta.   Ay, madam, let him compass   60
Whole parks and forests, as great rangers do;
At roosting time a little lodge can hold 'em.
Earth-conquering Alexander, that thought the world
Too narrow for him, in the end had but his pit-hole.
Beatrice. I fear thou art not modest, Diaphanta.   65
Diaphanta. Your thoughts are so unwilling to be known,
    madam;
'Tis ever the bride's fashion towards bed-time
To set light by her joys as if she owed 'em not.
Beatrice. Her joys? Her fears, thou wouldst say.
Diaphanta.   Fear of what?
Beatrice. Art thou a maid, and talk'st so to a maid?   70
You leave a blushing business behind,
Beshrew your heart for't!
Diaphanta.   Do you mean good sooth, madam?
Beatrice. Well, if I'd thought upon the fear at first,
Man should have been unknown.
Diaphanta.   Is't possible?

55–6. *'tis . . . purchase*] only a very scrupulous girl cannot be bribed with
gold.

57. *look*] look for.

60. *compass*] ride round, travel through.

61. *rangers*] (1) keepers of the parks; (2) rakes.

62. *lodge*] hunting-lodge, small hut (but also vagina, place to lodge the
penis).

63. *Alexander*] Alexander the Great (356–323 BC); lines 63–4 may echo
Juvenal, *Satire X*, 168–72.

64. *pit-hole*] (1) grave; (2) woman's vagina.

68. *owed*] owned.

71.] Beatrice pretends to be deeply embarrassed by Diaphanta's ribald
comments.

72. *Do . . . sooth*] Are you really speaking the truth?

74. *man . . . unknown*] either (1) 'I would have wished that the male sex did
not exist', or (2) 'I would have decided to remain a virgin'.

Beatrice. I will give a thousand ducats to that woman   75
    Would try what my fear were, and tell me true
    Tomorrow when she gets from't; as she likes,
    I might perhaps be drawn to't.
Diaphanta.   Are you in earnest?
Beatrice. Do you get the woman, then challenge me,
    And see if I'll fly from't; but I must tell you   80
    This by the way, she must be a true maid,
    Else there's no trial; my fears are not hers else.
Diaphanta. Nay, she that I would put into your hands,
    madam,
    Shall be a maid.
Beatrice.   You know I should be shamed else,
    Because she lies for me.
Diaphanta.   'Tis a strange humour.   85
    But are you serious still? Would you resign
    Your first night's pleasure, and give money too?
Beatrice. As willingly as live. [*Aside*] Alas, the gold
    Is but a by-bet to wedge in the honour.
Diaphanta. I do not know how the world goes abroad   90
    For faith or honesty; there's both required in this.
    Madam, what say you to me, and stray no further?
    I've a good mind, in troth, to earn your money.
Beatrice. You're too quick, I fear, to be a maid.
Diaphanta. How? Not a maid? Nay, then you urge me,
    madam;   95
    Your honourable self is not a truer

---

76. *Would . . . were*] who would experience what I am so afraid of.

81. *true maid*] genuine virgin.

82. *my . . . else*] if she is not a virgin, she will not have the same anxieties as me.

85. *lies*] (1) lies down to make love; (2) tells lies.

humour] whim, caprice.

89. *by-bet*] side-bet, side issue. Diaphanta is surprised that Beatrice should not only be willing to give up her wedding night to another woman, but will even pay her for it. Beatrice makes it clear, in this aside, that the money is a minor matter compared to the preservation of her 'honour' (reputation).

90–1. *I . . . honesty*] i.e. I do not know how much trustworthiness or chastity can be found in the world nowadays.

94. *quick*] lively, vivacious.

95. *urge*] provoke, insult.

With all your fears upon you—
Beatrice. [*Aside*]   Bad enough then.
Diaphanta. Than I with all my lightsome joys about me.
Beatrice. I'm glad to hear't. Then you dare put your honesty
    Upon an easy trial?
Diaphanta.   Easy? Anything.   100
Beatrice. I'll come to you straight.   [*She goes to the closet.*]
Diaphanta. [*Aside*]   She will not search me, will she,
    Like the forewoman of a female jury?
Beatrice. Glass M: ay, this is it. Look, Diaphanta,
    You take no worse than I do.   [*She drinks.*]
Diaphanta.   And in so doing
    I will not question what 'tis, but take it.   [*She drinks.*]   105
Beatrice. [*Aside*] Now if the experiment be true, 'twill praise
    itself,
    And give me noble ease.—Begins already;
                    [*Diaphanta gapes.*]
    There's the first symptom; and what haste it makes
    To fall into the second, there by this time!
                   [*Diaphanta sneezes.*]
    Most admirable secret! On the contrary,   110
    It stirs not me a whit, which most concerns it.
Diaphanta. Ha, ha, ha!
Beatrice. [*Aside*]   Just in all things and in order
    As if 'twere circumscribed; one accident
    Gives way unto another.
Diaphanta.   Ha, ha, ha!
Beatrice.   How now, wench?
Diaphanta. Ha, ha, ha! I am so, so light at heart—ha, ha,
    ha!—so pleasurable!   115

---

97. *Bad . . . then*] if Diaphanta is no more chaste than Beatrice she must be pretty bad.

98. *lightsome*] lighthearted, cheerful.

101–2. *She . . . jury?*] an allusion to the notorious divorce trial of the Countess of Essex in 1613. The Countess sued for divorce on the grounds of non-consummation of the marriage, and during the trial was examined by a group of matrons and noblewomen.

106. *praise itself*] show its excellence.

111. *which . . . it*] I who am the person it most needs to test.

113. *circumscribed*] confined within strict limits, carefully specified.
accident] symptom.

But one swig more, sweet madam.
Beatrice.   Ay, tomorrow;
    We shall have time to sit by't.
Diaphanta.   Now I'm sad again.
Beatrice. [*Aside*] It lays itself so gently, too! [*To Diaphanta*]
    Come, wench,
    Most honest Diaphanta I dare call thee now.
Diaphanta. Pray tell me, madam, what trick call you this?   120
Beatrice. I'll tell thee all hereafter; we must study
    The carriage of this business.
Diaphanta.   I shall carry't well,
    Because I love the burden.
Beatrice.   About midnight
    You must not fail to steal forth gently,
    That I may use the place.
Diaphanta.   Oh, fear not, madam,   125
    I shall be cool by that time. [*Aside*] The bride's place,
    And with a thousand ducats! I'm for a justice now.
    I bring a portion with me; I scorn small fools.   *Exeunt.*

[IV. ii]

Enter VERMANDERO *and* Servant.

Vermandero. I tell thee, knave, mine honour is in question,
    A thing till now free from suspicion,
    Nor ever was there cause. Who of my gentlemen
    Are absent? Tell me and truly how many and who.
Servant. Antonio, sir, and Franciscus.   5
Vermandero. When did they leave the castle?
Servant. Some ten days since, sir, the one intending to
    Briamata, th'other for Valencia.

---

117. *to sit by't*] to sit and enjoy its effects at leisure.

118. *lays itself*] subsides, comes to an end.

122. *carriage*] way it is to be carried out (but Diaphanta plays on 'carry' as meaning 'undergo copulation').

127–8.] Having a dowry, I now intend to marry a big fool, a justice of the peace.

IV.ii.8. *Briamata*] In the main source of the play, Reynolds's *God's Revenge*, Briamata is a country estate belonging to Vermandero.

Vermandero. The time accuses 'em. A charge of murder
    Is brought within my castle gate, Piracquo's murder;   10
    I dare not answer faithfully their absence.
    A strict command of apprehension
    Shall pursue 'em suddenly, and either wipe
    The stain off clear or openly discover it.
    Provide me wingèd warrants for the purpose.   15
                           Exit Servant.
    See, I am set on again.

               Enter TOMAZO.

Tomazo. I claim a brother of you.
Vermandero.   You're too hot.
    Seek him not here.
Tomazo.   Yes, 'mongst your dearest bloods,
    If my peace find no fairer satisfaction.
    This is the place must yield account for him,   20
    For here I left him, and the hasty tie
    Of this snatched marriage gives strong testimony
    Of his most certain ruin.
Vermandero.   Certain falsehood!
    This is the place indeed; his breach of faith
    Has too much marred both my abusèd love,   25
    The honourable love I reserved for him,
    And mocked my daughter's joy. The prepared morning
    Blushed at his infidelity; he left
    Contempt and scorn to throw upon those friends
    Whose belief hurt 'em. Oh, 'twas most ignoble   30
    To take his flight so unexpectedly,
    And throw such public wrongs on those that loved him.

---

    11. *answer faithfully*] explain confidently, in good faith.

    12. *apprehension*] arrest.

    14. *discover*] reveal.

    16. *set on*] about to be attacked (he has noticed the entrance of Tomazo).

    18. *bloods*] blood relations (and also implying that he will shed their blood).

    20. *must*] that must.

    22. *snatched*] sudden, hurried.

    25. *marred*] injured.

    30. *Whose . . . 'em*] who were embarrassed because they had believed in his trustworthiness.

Tomazo. Then this is all your answer?
Vermandero.   'Tis too fair
    For one of his alliance; and I warn you
    That this place no more see you.   *Exit.*

Enter DE FLORES.

Tomazo.   The best is,   35
    There is more ground to meet a man's revenge on.—
    Honest De Flores!
De Flores.   That's my name indeed.
    Saw you the bride? Good sweet sir, which way took she?
Tomazo. I have blest mine eyes from seeing such a false one.
De Flores. [*Aside*] I'd fain get off; this man's not for my
    company;   40
    I smell his brother's blood when I come near him.
Tomazo. Come hither, kind and true one; I remember
    My brother loved thee well.
De Flores.   Oh, purely, dear sir!
    [*Aside*] Methinks I am now again a-killing on him,
    He brings it so fresh to me.
Tomazo.   Thou canst guess, sirrah,   45
    (One honest friend has an instinct of jealousy)
    At some foul guilty person?
De Flores. 'Las, sir, I am so charitable, I think none
    Worse than myself. You did not see the bride then?
Tomazo. I prithee name her not. Is she not wicked?   50
De Flores. No, no, a pretty, easy, round-packed sinner,
    As your most ladies are, else you might think
    I flattered her; but, sir, at no hand wicked,
    Till they're so old their chins and noses meet,
    And they salute witches. I am called, I think, sir. 55

---

34. *alliance*] kindred, family.
35. *That . . . you*] not to come here again.
36. *ground . . . on*] ways of obtaining revenge.
43. *purely*] wholeheartedly.
46. *instinct of jealousy*] instinctive suspicion.
51. *round-packed*] possibly meaning 'plump, shapely'.
52. *As . . . are*] as most ladies are.
53. *at no hand*] by no means.
55. *salute*] are given the title of.
I am called] Someone is calling for me.

[*Aside*] His company ev'n o'erlays my conscience.

Exit.

Tomazo. That De Flores has a wondrous honest heart;
    He'll bring it out in time, I'm assured on't.
    Oh, here's the glorious master of the day's joy.
    'Twill not be long till he and I do reckon.   60

Enter ALSEMERO.

    Sir!

Alsemero. You are most welcome.

Tomazo.   You may call that word back;
    I do not think I am, nor wish to be.

Alsemero. 'Tis strange you found the way to this house, then.

Tomazo. Would I'd ne'er known the cause! I'm none of
      those, sir,
    That come to give you joy, and swill your wine;   65
    'Tis a more precious liquor that must lay
    The fiery thirst I bring.

Alsemero.   Your words and you
    Appear to me great strangers.

Tomazo.   Time and our swords
    May make us more acquainted. This the business:
    I should have a brother in your place;   70
    How treachery and malice have disposed of him,
    I'm bound to enquire of him which holds his right,
    Which never could come fairly.

Alsemero.   You must look
    To answer for that word, sir.

Tomazo.   Fear you not,
    I'll have it ready drawn at our next meeting.   75

---

56. *o'erlays*] weighs down, oppresses.

58. *it*] the truth about Alonzo.

59. *glorious*] said ironically; the word can also mean proud, vainglorious.

60. *reckon*] settle accounts, fight.

66. *liquor*] i.e. blood.

    lay] allay, quench.

67–8. *Your . . . strangers*] Your unexpected words and behaviour seem very strange to me.

72. *his right*] Beatrice, who rightfully belonged to Alonzo.

73. *fairly*] honestly, without trickery.

75. *it . . . drawn*] (1) my answer drawn up; (2) my sword drawn.

Keep your day solemn. Farewell, I disturb it not;
I'll bear the smart with patience for a time.   *Exit.*
Alsemero. 'Tis somewhat ominous this, a quarrel entered
Upon this day. My innocence relieves me;

Enter JASPERINO.

I should be wondrous sad else.—Jasperino,   80
I have news to tell thee, strange news.
Jasperino.   I ha' some too,
I think as strange as yours; would I might keep
Mine, so my faith and friendship might be kept in't!
Faith, sir, dispense a little with my zeal,
And let it cool in this.
Alsemero.   This puts me on,   85
And blames thee for thy slowness.
Jasperino.   All may prove nothing;
Only a friendly fear that leapt from me, sir.
Alsemero. No question it may prove nothing; let's partake it,
   though.
Jasperino. 'Twas Diaphanta's chance (for to that wench
I pretend honest love, and she deserves it)   90
To leave me in a back part of the house,
A place we chose for private conference.
She was no sooner gone but instantly
I heard your bride's voice in the next room to me;
And lending more attention, found De Flores   95
Louder than she.
Alsemero.   De Flores? Thou art out now.
Jasperino. You'll tell me more anon.
Alsemero.   Still I'll prevent thee;

---

76. *Keep . . . solemn*] Celebrate your day of marriage with due ceremony.
77. *smart*] pain, grief.
82. *keep*] keep back, conceal.
83. *so*] provided that.
84–5. *dispense . . . this*] i.e. allow me not to be so zealous in your service as
I usually am, so that I may keep back this news.
85. *puts me on*] incites me, makes me keener to hear you.
88. *partake*] share, learn.
90. *pretend*] offer.
96. *out*] mistaken.
97. *You'll . . . anon*] You'll soon talk differently.
prevent] forestall.

The very sight of him is poison to her.

Jasperino. That made me stagger too, but Diaphanta
At her return confirmed it.

Alsemero.   Diaphanta!   100

Jasperino. Then fell we both to listen, and words passed
Like those that challenge interest in a woman.

Alsemero. Peace, quench thy zeal; 'tis dangerous to thy
bosom.

Jasperino. Then truth is full of peril.

Alsemero.   Such truths are.
Oh, were she the sole glory of the earth,   105
Had eyes that could shoot fire into kings' breasts,
And touched, she sleeps not here! Yet I have time,
Though night be near, to be resolved hereof;
And prithee do not weigh me by my passions.

Jasperino. I never weighed friend so.

Alsemero.   Done charitably.   110
That key will lead thee to a pretty secret, [*Giving a key*]
By a Chaldean taught me, and I've made
My study upon some. Bring from my closet
A glass inscribed there with the letter M,
And question not my purpose.

Jasperino.   It shall be done, sir.   115

                                        Exit.

Alsemero. How can this hang together? Not an hour since,
Her woman came pleading her lady's fears,
Delivered her for the most timorous virgin
That ever shrunk at man's name, and so modest

---

99. *stagger*] hesitate, doubt myself.

101. *fell we both*] we both proceeded.

102. *challenge interest*] claim a right or share (possibly they overheard De Flores claiming his reward from Beatrice in III.iv).

107. *touched*] tainted, unchaste.
here] in my bed.

108. *to be . . . hereof*] to settle this question.

109 *weigh . . . passions*] judge me by my outbursts of strong feeling.

111. *pretty*] ingenious, admirable.

112. *Chaldean*] soothsayer, astrologer (see Daniel, 2).

116. *Not . . . since*] less than an hour ago.

118. *Delivered her for*] described her as.

She charged her weep out her request to me   120
That she might come obscurely to my bosom.

Enter BEATRICE-JOANNA.

Beatrice. [*Aside*] All things go well; my woman's preparing
    yonder
  For her sweet voyage, which grieves me to lose.
  Necessity compels it; I lose all else.
Alsemero. [*Aside*] Push, modesty's shrine is set in yonder
    forehead.   125
  I cannot be too sure, though. [*To her*] My Joanna!
Beatrice. Sir, I was bold to weep a message to you;
  Pardon my modest fears.
Alsemero. [*Aside*]   The dove's not meeker;
  She's abused, questionless.

Enter JASPERINO [*with glass*].

               —Oh, are you come, sir?
Beatrice. [*Aside*] The glass, upon my life! I see the letter.   130
Jasperino. Sir, this is M.
Alsemero.   'Tis it.
Beatrice. [*Aside*]   I am suspected.
Alsemero. How fitly our bride comes to partake with us!
Beatrice. What is't, my lord?
Alsemero.   No hurt.
Beatrice.   Sir, pardon me;
  I seldom taste of any composition.
Alsemero. But this upon my warrant you shall venture on.   135
Beatrice. I fear 'twill make me ill.
Alsemero.   Heaven forbid that
Beatrice. [*Aside*] I'm put now to my cunning; th'effects I
    know,
  If I can now but feign 'em handsomely.   [*She drinks.*]

---

121. *obscurely*] in darkness; Beatrice is preparing for the substitution of
Diaphanta for herself.
129. *She's . . . questionless*] she has definitely been maligned.
134. *composition*] medicine made of mixed ingredients.
135. *warrant*] guarantee (that it is harmless).
138. *handsomely*] effectively.

Alsemero. [*To Jasperino*] It has that secret virtue—it ne'er
    missed, sir—
    Upon a virgin.
Jasperino.   Treble qualitied?   140
                [*Beatrice-Joanna gapes, then sneezes.*]
Alsemero. By all that's virtuous, it takes there, proceeds!
Jasperino. This is the strangest trick to know a maid by.
Beatrice. Ha, ha, ha!
    You have given me joy of heart to drink, my lord.
Alsemero. No, thou hast given me such joy of heart   145
    That never can be blasted.
Beatrice.   What's the matter, sir?
Alsemero. [*To Jasperino*] See, now 'tis settled in a melancholy,
    Keeps both the time and method. [*To her*] My Joanna!
    Chaste as the breath of heaven, or morning's womb,
    That brings the day forth; thus my love encloses thee.   150
                [*He embraces her.*] *Exeunt.*

[IV. iii]

        Enter ISABELLA [*with a letter*] *and* LOLLIO.

Isabella. O heaven! Is this the waxing moon?
    Does love turn fool, run mad, and all at once?
    Sirrah, here's a madman, akin to the fool too,
    A lunatic lover.
Lollio. No, no, not he I brought the letter from?   5
Isabella. Compare his inside with his out, and tell me.
                [*She gives him the letter.*]
Lollio. The out's mad, I'm sure of that; I had a taste on't. [*He*

---

    140. *Treble qualitied*] with three powers or effects.
    141. *takes*] takes effect.
    146. *blasted*] blighted, destroyed.
    148. *Keeps . . . method*] The drug has produced the correct sequence of
responses.

    IV.iii.1. *waxing*] increasing in size (and becoming more powerful).
    6. *Compare . . . out*] i.e. Compare the contents of the letter with what is
written on the cover of it.

reads.] 'To the bright Andromeda, chief chambermaid
to the Knight of the Sun, at the sign of Scorpio, in the
middle region, sent by the bellows mender of Aeolus. Pay   10
the post.' This is stark madness.

Isabella. Now mark the inside. [*She takes the letter and reads*.]
'Sweet lady, having now cast off this counterfeit cover of
a madman, I appear to your best judgement a true and
faithful lover of your beauty.'   15

Lollio. He is mad still.

Isabella. 'If any fault you find, chide those perfections in you,
which have made me imperfect; 'tis the same sun that
causeth to grow and enforceth to wither—'

Lollio. Oh, rogue!   20

Isabella. '—Shapes and transshapes, destroys and builds
again. I come in winter to you dismantled of my proper
ornaments; by the sweet splendour of your cheerful
smiles, I spring and live a lover.'

Lollio. Mad rascal still!   25

Isabella. 'Tread him not under foot, that shall appear an honour to your bounties. I remain—mad till I speak with you,
from whom I expect my cure. Yours all, or one beside
himself, Franciscus.'

Lollio. You are like to have a fine time on't. My master and I   30
may give over our professions; I do not think but you can

8–11.] Isabella is addressed as Andromeda because Franciscus is the
Perseus who will rescue her from the dragon Alibius. Chambermaids were
often regarded as lascivious, and fond of reading chivalric romances such as
The Mirror of Knighthood, a translation from Spanish published in nine parts
between 1578 and 1601, in which one of the heroes is named the Knight of
the Sun. Scorpio was the sign governing the privy parts of the body, and this
turns 'middle region', an astronomical term, into an obvious pun. Aeolus
was the god of winds.

11. *post*] bearer of the letter.

18. *made me imperfect*] forced me to appear much less impressive than I
normally am.

22–3. *dismantled . . . ornaments*] not wearing my own clothes and
accessories.

26–7. *that . . . bounties*] who will show himself to be an honourable gentleman if you are generous to him.

28–9. *beside himself*] distracted with love.

31. *I . . . but*] I am sure that.

cure fools and madmen faster than we, with little pains
too.

Isabella. Very likely.

Lollio. One thing I must tell you, mistress. You perceive that   35
I am privy to your skill; if I find you minister once and set
up the trade, I put in for my thirds. I shall be mad or fool
else.

Isabella. The first place is thine, believe it, Lollio;
If I do fall—   40

Lollio. I fall upon you.

Isabella. So.

Lollio. Well, I stand to my venture.

Isabella. But thy counsel now. How shall I deal with 'em?

Lollio. Why, do you mean to deal with 'em?   45

Isabella. Nay, the fair understanding: how to use 'em.

Lollio. Abuse 'em! That's the way to mad the fool, and make
a fool of the madman, and then you use 'em kindly.

Isabella. 'Tis easy, I'll practise; do thou observe it.
The key of thy wardrobe.   50

Lollio. There; fit yourself for 'em, and I'll fit 'em both for you.
[*He gives her the key.*]

Isabella. Take thou no further notice than the outside.
   Exit.

Lollio. Not an inch; I'll put you to the inside.

---

36. *am privy to*] know about.
  minister] (1) provide medical treatment; (2) respond to your lover.
37. *I put in for*] I shall apply for, expect from you.
  thirds] literally a third of the proceeds of captures, or of certain fines, etc.,
of which two-thirds were due to the king. Lollio wants a third for himself,
and the other two-thirds would go to Alibius and whichever lover Isabella
chooses.
40–1. *fall . . . fall upon*] yield to a lover . . . leap upon sexually.
43. *stand to*] (with erotic double meaning).
46. *fair*] decent, modest (she rebukes Lollio for his obscene interpretation
of her question).
47. *Abuse*] cheat, deceive.
48. *kindly*] (1) affectionately; (2) in the way appropriate to them.
49. *practise*] carry it out.
52.] i.e. Treat me as though I really was a madwoman.
53. *I'll . . . inside*] This may mean 'I'll allow you intimate access to your
lovers'.

Enter ALIBIUS.

Alibius. Lollio, art there? Will all be perfect, think'st thou?
　　Tomorrow night, as if to close up the solemnity,　　　　55
　　Vermandero expects us.
Lollio. I mistrust the madmen most. The fools will do well
　　enough; I have taken pains with them.
Alibius. Tush, they cannot miss; the more absurdity,
　　The more commends it—so no rough behaviours　　　　60
　　Affright the ladies. They are nice things, thou know'st.
Lollio. You need not fear, sir; so long as we are there with our
　　commanding pizzles, they'll be as tame as the ladies
　　themselves.
Alibius. I will see them once more rehearse before they go.　　　65
Lollio. I was about it, sir; look you to the madmen's morris,
　　and let me alone with the other. There is one or two that
　　I mistrust their fooling; I'll instruct them, and then they
　　shall rehearse the whole measure.
Alibius. Do so; I'll see the music prepared. But Lollio,　　　70
　　By the way, how does my wife brook her restraint?
　　Does she not grudge at it?
Lollio. So, so; she takes some pleasure in the house, she would
　　abroad else. You must allow her a little more length; she's
　　kept too short.　　　　75
Alibius. She shall along to Vermandero's with us;
　　That will serve her for a month's liberty.
Lollio. What's that on your face, sir?
Alibius. Where, Lollio? I see nothing.

---

55. *solemnity*] festivity.
57. *mistrust*] am worried about.
60. *so*] so long as.
61. *nice*] delicate, fastidious.
63. *pizzles*] bulls' penises, used as whips.
66-7. *look . . . other*] you must supervise the madmen who are dancing, and leave me to attend to the fools who are dancing.
66. *morris*] morris dance, an English folk dance.
67-8. *There . . . fooling*] Lollio suspects that Antonio and Franciscus will 'fool about' in the wrong way if they are not watched.
69. *measure*] dance.
71. *brook*] endure, tolerate.
72. *grudge*] complain.

Lollio. Cry you mercy, sir, 'tis your nose; it showed like the   80
    trunk of a young elephant.

Alibius. Away, rascal! I'll prepare the music, Lollio.

                             Exit ALIBIUS.

Lollio. Do, sir, and I'll dance the whilst.—Tony, where art
    thou, Tony?

                  Enter ANTONIO.

Antonio. Here, cousin; where art thou?   85

Lollio. Come, Tony, the footmanship I taught you.

Antonio. I had rather ride, cousin.

Lollio. Ay, a whip take you; but I'll keep you out. Vault in;
    look you, Tony: fa, la la, la la.   [*He dances.*]

Antonio. Fa, la la, la la.   [*He dances.*]   90

Lollio. There, an honour.

Antonio. Is this an honour, coz?   [*He bows.*]

Lollio. Yes, an it please your worship.

Antonio. Does honour bend in the hams, coz?

Lollio. Marry does it; as low as worship, squireship, nay,   95
    yeomanry itself sometimes, from whence it first stiffened.
    There rise, a caper.

Antonio. Caper after an honour, coz?

Lollio. Very proper; for honour is but a caper, rises as fast and
    high, has a knee or two, and falls to the ground again.   100
    You can remember your figure, Tony?   *Exit.*

---

80. *Cry you mercy*] I beg your pardon.

80–1.] The long nose may be equivalent to the cuckold's horns, or it may
mean that Alibius is being led by the nose.

87. *ride*] See line 153 below.

88. *I'll keep you out*] perhaps meaning 'I'll keep you from getting what you
want'.

91. *honour*] bow or curtsy (but in lines 94–100 Lollio and Antonio play on
the sense of the word as 'high social status').

94. *hams*] hips.

95. *Marry does it*] indeed it does.

worship] important people (who would be addressed as 'your worship', as
in line 93).

95–6.] This seems to be an attack on upstarts who rise to great prominence
from relatively modest backgrounds by fawning.

96. *stiffened*] rose upward in a laborious way.

97. *caper*] wild leap in dancing.

99–100.] Advancement is sudden and capricious, has a brief period of
respect shown to it ('a knee or two'), and then collapses.

101–2. *figure . . . figure*] dance-figure, pattern of steps . . . face, appearance.

Antonio. Yes, cousin; when I see thy figure, I can remember
    mine.

        Enter ISABELLA [*like a madwoman*].

Isabella. Hey, how he treads the air! Shoo, shoo, t'other way!
    He burns his wings else; here's wax enough below,   105
    Icarus, more than will be cancelled these eighteen moons.
    He's down, he's down, what a terrible fall he had!
    Stand up, thou son of Cretan Daedalus,
    And let us tread the lower labyrinth;
    I'll bring thee to the clue.   110
Antonio. [*To Isabella*] Prithee, coz, let me alone.
Isabella. Art thou not drowned?
    About thy head I saw a heap of clouds,
    Wrapped like a Turkish turban; on thy back
    A crook'd chameleon-coloured rainbow hung   115
    Like a tiara down unto thy hams.
    Let me suck out those billows in thy belly;
    Hark how they roar and rumble in the straits!
    Bless thee from the pirates.
Antonio. Pox upon you, let me alone!   120
Isabella. Why shouldst thou mount so high as Mercury,
    Unless thou hadst reversion of his place?
    Stay in the moon with me, Endymion,

---

106. *Icarus*] son of Daedalus, a skilled craftsman who built the labyrinth at
Crete. Imprisoned in the labyrinth, father and son escaped by means of
artificial wings held together with wax. Icarus flew too near the sun, so that
the wax melted, and he fell into the sea and drowned.

    cancelled] Isabella is now thinking of wax used for seals on legal deeds.

110.] This brings in another story related to the labyrinth built by
Daedalus; *clue* refers to the thread Ariadne gave to Theseus so that he could
find his way out of the labyrinth after killing the minotaur (i.e. Alibius).

115. *chameleon-coloured*] As chameleons can change their colour to suit
their background, the term is deliberately nonsensical.

117. *those billows*] i.e. the sea water.

118. *straits*] presumably the sea between Crete and Greece, if Isabella is
still thinking in terms of the Icarus legend.

119. *Bless thee*] may heaven protect you.

121. *Mercury*] the messenger of the gods, often portrayed with winged
sandals.

122. *reversion*] promise of an office when the holder of it dies.

123. *Endymion*] a beautiful youth with whom Luna (the moon) fell in love.

And we will rule these wild rebellious waves
    That would have drowned my love.   125
Antonio. I'll kick thee if again thou touch me,
    Thou wild unshapen antic; I am no fool,
    You bedlam!
Isabella.   But you are, as sure as I am, mad.
    Have I put on this habit of a frantic,
    With love as full of fury to beguile   130
    The nimble eye of watchful jealousy,
    And am I thus rewarded?   *[She reveals herself.]*
Antonio. Ha! Dearest beauty!
Isabella.   No, I have no beauty now,
    Nor never had, but what was in my garments.
    You a quick-sighted lover? Come not near me!   135
    Keep your caparisons; you're aptly clad;
    I came a feigner to return stark mad.   *Exit.*

Enter LOLLIO.

Antonio. Stay, or I shall change condition
    And become as you are.
Lollio. Why, Tony, whither now? Why, fool?   140
Antonio. Whose fool, usher of idiots? You coxcomb!
    I have fooled too much.
Lollio. You were best be mad another while, then.
Antonio. So I am, stark mad; I have cause enough,
    And I could throw the full effects on thee   145
    And beat thee like a fury!
Lollio. Do not, do not; I shall not forbear the gentleman under
    the fool, if you do. Alas, I saw through your fox-skin

---

127. *unshapen*] deformed, ugly.
antic] grotesque performer.
136. *caparisons*] garish, brightly-coloured clothing.
you're aptly clad] you are dressed appropriately (because you really are a fool).
137.] i.e. I came in pretending to be mad, but am now going out mad in earnest.
138–9.] i.e. if you leave me I too will become mad in earnest.
141. *usher*] (1) doorkeeper; (2) assistant master, teacher.
147–8. *I . . . do*] I will not tolerate rough behaviour from you even if you are really a gentleman in disguise (perhaps an allusion to III.iii.145).
148. *fox-skin*] cunning disguise.

before now. Come, I can give you comfort; my mistress
loves you, and there is as arrant a madman i' th' house as   150
you are a fool, your rival, whom she loves not. If after the
masque we can rid her of him, you earn her love, she says,
and the fool shall ride her.

Antonio. May I believe thee?

Lollio. Yes, or you may choose whether you will or no.   155

Antonio. She's eased of him; I have a good quarrel on't.

Lollio. Well, keep your old station yet, and be quiet.

Antonio. Tell her I will deserve her love.   [*Exit.*]

Lollio. And you are like to have your desire.

Enter FRANCISCUS.

Franciscus. [*Sings*] 'Down, down, down a-down a-down,
    and then with a horse-trick,   160
  To kick Latona's forehead, and break her bowstring.'

Lollio. This is t'other counterfeit; I'll put him out of his humour. [*He takes out letter and reads.*] 'Sweet lady, having
now cast off this counterfeit cover of a madman, I appear
to your best judgement a true and faithful lover of your   165
beauty.' This is pretty well for a madman.

Franciscus. Ha! What's that?

Lollio. 'Chide those perfections in you, which have made me
imperfect.'

Franciscus. I am discovered to the fool.   170

Lollio. I hope to discover the fool in you, ere I have done with
you. 'Yours all, or one beside himself, Franciscus.' This
madman will mend, sure.

---

153. *ride*] make love to.

156. *She's . . . him*] I'll get rid of him for her.

a good quarrel on't] a valid reason for fighting him.

160. *Down . . . a-down*] common in song and ballad refrains, with no
precise meaning.

horse-trick] ?violent leap or movement (perhaps imitating a performing
horse).

161. *Latona*] mother of the twin gods Apollo and Diana, but referring here
to Diana herself. She was a huntress, and the 'bowstring' would belong to her
bow. (Probably another concealed reference to Isabella.)

170. *discovered*] revealed.

the fool] i.e. Lollio. (The line may be spoken as an aside, but Lollio
overhears and replies to it.)

Franciscus. What do you read, sirrah?

Lollio. Your destiny, sir; you'll be hanged for this trick, and   175
    another that I know.

Franciscus. Art thou of counsel with thy mistress?

Lollio. Next her apron strings.

Franciscus. Give me thy hand.

Lollio. Stay, let me put yours in my pocket first. [*He puts away*   180
    the letter.] Your hand is true, is it not? It will not pick? I
    partly fear it, because I think it does lie.

Franciscus. Not in a syllable.

Lollio. So; if you love my mistress so well as you have handled
    the matter here, you are like to be cured of your madness.   185

Franciscus. And none but she can cure it.

Lollio. Well, I'll give you over then, and she shall cast your
    water next.

Franciscus. Take for thy pains past.   [*He gives him money.*]

Lollio. I shall deserve more, sir, I hope; my mistress loves you,   190
    but must have some proof of your love to her.

Franciscus. There I meet my wishes.

Lollio. That will not serve; you must meet her enemy and
    yours.

Franciscus. He's dead already!   195

Lollio. Will you tell me that, and I parted but now with him?

Franciscus. Show me the man.

Lollio. Ay, that's a right course now, see him before you kill
    him in any case, and yet it needs not go so far neither; 'tis

---

175. *this trick*] the letter.

176. *another*] possibly the 'horse-trick' of line 160, interpreted obscenely
by Lollio.

177. *of counsel with*] in the confidence of.

180. *yours*] Lollio plays on the alternative sense of *hand* as 'handwriting,
letter'.

181. *Your . . . true*] (1) You are not a pickpocket; (2) Your letter contains
the truth.

pick] pick pockets.

187. *give you over*] stop trying to cure you.

187–8. *cast your water*] examine your urine as a diagnosis.

192.] That is what I most want to do.

195.] i.e. He's as good as dead already (but Lollio interprets it literally).

196. *but now*] just now.

198–9. *see him . . . kill him*] identify your victim before killing him (Lollio
continues to deflate the language used by Franciscus).

but a fool that haunts the house and my mistress in the   200
shape of an idiot. Bang but his fool's coat well-
favouredly, and 'tis well.

Franciscus. Soundly, soundly!

Lollio. Only reserve him till the masque be past, and if you
find him not now in the dance yourself, I'll show you. In,   205
in! My master!

Franciscus. He handles him like a feather.—Hey!

                              [*Exit dancing.*]

                    Enter ALIBIUS.

Alibius. Well said; in a readiness, Lollio?

Lollio. Yes, sir.

Alibius. Away then, and guide them in, Lollio;   210
Entreat your mistress to see this sight.   [*Exit* LOLLIO.]
Hark, is there not one incurable fool
That might be begged? I have friends.

Lollio. [*Within*] I have him for you, one that shall deserve it
too.   215

Alibius. Good boy, Lollio.

    [*Enter* ISABELLA, *then* LOLLIO *with* Madmen *and* Fools.]
            The Madmen and Fools dance.

'Tis perfect. Well, fit but once these strains,
We shall have coin and credit for our pains.   *Exeunt.*

201–2. *Bang . . . well-favouredly*] i.e. thrash Antonio soundly.

204. *reserve*] spare.

206. *My master*] Lollio notices the approach of Alibius.

208. *Well said*] well done.

212–13.] To beg a fool was to petition the Court of Wards for the custody
of an idiot and his estates. The process was riddled with favouritism and
corruption, and was abolished at the Restoration. If Alibius can be appointed
guardian of one of his patients he will gain control of the patient's property.

213. *friends*] powerful patrons who could influence decisions made by the
Court of Wards.

214. *him*] Antonio.

217. *fit . . . strains*] if we can organise dancing appropriate to the music
(i.e. ensure that all goes well on the night of the wedding entertainment).

Act V

Enter BEATRICE-JOANNA. *A clock strikes one.*

Beatrice. One struck, and yet she lies by't!—O my fears!
    This strumpet serves her own ends, 'tis apparent now,
    Devours the pleasure with a greedy appetite,
    And never minds my honour or my peace,
    Makes havoc of my right; but she pays dearly for't: 5
    No trusting of her life with such a secret,
    That cannot rule her blood to keep her promise.
    Beside, I have some suspicion of her faith to me,
    Because I was suspected of my lord,
    And it must come from her.—Hark, by my horrors!   10
    Another clock strikes two.   *Strikes two.*

Enter DE FLORES.

De Flores.   Psst! Where are you?
Beatrice. De Flores?
De Flores.   Ay; is she not come from him yet?
Beatrice. As I am a living soul, not.
De Flores.   Sure the devil
    Hath sowed his itch within her. Who'd trust
    A waiting-woman?
Beatrice.   I must trust somebody.   15
De Flores. Push, they are termagants,
    Especially when they fall upon their masters,

    V.i.1. *lies by't*] 'Lie by it' can mean 'lie in prison'; Diaphanta is still
enclosed with Alsemero.
    4. *peace*] peace of mind.
    8.] i.e. I suspect that she has been disloyal to me (and betrayed my secrets
to Alsemero).
    9. *of*] by.
    14. *itch*] obsessive desire to commit evil (in this case sexual).
    16. *termagants*] fierce, violent women.
    17. *fall upon*] encounter sexually.

And have their ladies' first-fruits. They're mad whelps;
You cannot stave 'em off from game royal. Then
You are so harsh and hardy, ask no counsel,   20
And I could have helped you to an apothecary's daughter,
Would have fall'n off before eleven, and thanked you too.
Beatrice. Oh, me, not yet? This whore forgets herself.
De Flores. The rascal fares so well. Look, you're undone;
    The day-star, by this hand! See Phosphorus plain yonder. 25
Beatrice. Advise me now to fall upon some ruin;
    There is no counsel safe else.
De Flores.   Peace, I ha't now,
    For we must force a rising; there's no remedy.
Beatrice. How? Take heed of that.
De Flores.   Tush, be you quiet,
    Or else give over all.
Beatrice.   Prithee, I ha' done then.   30
De Flores. This is my reach: I'll set some part afire
    Of Diaphanta's chamber.
Beatrice.   How? Fire, sir?
    That may endanger the whole house.
De Flores. You talk of danger when your fame's on fire?
Beatrice. That's true; do what thou wilt now.
De Flores.   Push, I aim   35
    At a most rich success, strikes all dead sure.
    The chimney being afire, and some light parcels
    Of the least danger in her chamber only,

---

18. *first-fruits*] first passionate love-making by the husband.

18–19. *They're . . . royal*] They are like frenzied young dogs, who cannot be prevented from hunting game reserved for the king.

20. *harsh and hardy*] rough and rash (foolhardy).
counsel] advice.

22. *Would . . . off*] who would have stopped.

25. *Phosphorus*] the morning-star, Venus.

26. *fall . . . ruin*] happen upon, or devise, some catastrophe.

28. *force a rising*] create a disturbance to wake the house.

30. *give over all*] give up any hope of success.

31. *reach*] scheme.

34. *fame*] reputation.

36. *strikes . . . sure*] which makes everything completely safe.

37–8. *and some . . . only*] i.e. There are only a few small packages in her room, which would be unlikely to set fire to the whole house.

If Diaphanta should be met by chance then,
Far from her lodging (which is now suspicious),   40
It would be thought her fears and affrights then
Drove her to seek for succour; if not seen
Or met at all, as that's the likeliest,
For her own shame she'll hasten towards her lodging.
I will be ready with a piece high-charged,   45
As 'twere to cleanse the chimney; there 'tis proper now,
But she shall be the mark.
Beatrice.   I'm forced to love thee now,
  'Cause thou provid'st so carefully for my honour.
De Flores. 'Slid, it concerns the safety of us both,
  Our pleasure and continuance.
Beatrice.   One word now, prithee: 50
  How for the servants?
De Flores.   I'll dispatch them
  Some one way, some another in the hurry,
  For buckets, hooks, ladders; fear not you.
  The deed shall find its time; and I've thought since
  Upon a safe conveyance for the body too.   55
  How this fire purifies wit! Watch you your minute.
Beatrice. Fear keeps my soul upon't; I cannot stray from't.

        Enter ALONZO'S GHOST.

De Flores. Ha! What art thou that tak'st away the light
  'Twixt that star and me? I dread thee not;
  'Twas but a mist of conscience.—All's clear again.   60
                                  Exit.
Beatrice. Who's that, De Flores? Bless me! It slides by;
                             [*Exit* GHOST.]
  Some ill thing haunts the house; 't has left behind it
  A shivering sweat upon me. I'm afraid now.

---

45. *piece high-charged*] heavily-loaded gun.

46. *proper*] fitting.

47. *mark*] target.

49. *'Slid*] an oath (abbreviation of 'by God's eyelid').

50. *continuance*] Beatrice's infidelity has now become habitual.

54. *The deed . . . time*] i.e. I will kill Diaphanta when the time is right.

56. *purifies wit*] stimulates my ingenuity.

57. *stray from't*] let my thoughts wander from it (the right moment to rejoin Alsemero).

This night hath been so tedious; oh, this strumpet!
Had she a thousand lives, he should not leave her   65
Till he had destroyed the last.—List, oh my terrors!
Three struck by Saint Sebastian's!   *Struck three o'clock.*
Within. Fire, fire, fire!
Beatrice. Already? How rare is that man's speed!
How heartily he serves me! His face loathes one,   70
But look upon his care, who would not love him?
The east is not more beauteous than his service.
Within. Fire, fire, fire!

Enter DE FLORES; Servants *pass over, ring a bell.*

De Flores. Away, dispatch! Hooks, buckets, ladders; that's
    well said.
The fire-bell rings, the chimney works; my charge;   75
The piece is ready.   *Exit.*
Beatrice.   Here's a man worth loving—

Enter DIAPHANTA.

Oh, you're a jewel!
Diaphanta.   Pardon frailty, madam;
In troth I was so well, I ev'n forgot myself.
Beatrice. You've made trim work.
Diaphanta.   What?
Beatrice.   Hie quickly to your chamber;
Your reward follows you.
Diaphanta.   I never made   80
So sweet a bargain.   *Exit.*

Enter ALSEMERO.

Alsemero.   Oh, my dear Joanna,
Alas, art thou risen too? I was coming,

65–6. *Had she . . . last*] Apparently expressing contempt for Diaphanta's
voracious sexual appetite.

67. *Saint Sebastian's*] the clock in St Sebastian's church.

69. *rare*] (1) excellent; (2) unusual.

70. *loathes*] disgusts.

71. *his care*] the care he takes.

72. *The east*] dawn, sunrise.

75. *my charge*] I must carry out my task.

79. *You've . . . work*] You've done a nice job (sarcastic).

My absolute treasure.
Beatrice.   When I missed you,
    I could not choose but follow.
Alsemero.   Thou'rt all sweetness!
    The fire is not so dangerous.
Beatrice.   Think you so, sir?   85
Alsemero. I prithee tremble not; believe me, 'tis not.

            Enter VERMANDERO *and* JASPERINO.

Vermandero. Oh, bless my house and me!
Alsemero.   My lord your father.

            Enter DE FLORES *with a piece.*

Vermandero. Knave, whither goes that piece?
De Flores.   To scour the chimney.
                                                Exit.
Vermandero. Oh, well said, well said;
    That fellow's good on all occasions.   90
Beatrice. A wondrous necessary man, my lord.
Vermandero. He hath a ready wit; he's worth 'em all, sir.
    Dog at a house of fire; I ha' seen him singed ere now.
                                        The piece goes off.
    Ha, there he goes.
Beatrice. [*Aside*]   'Tis done.
Alsemero.   Come, sweet, to bed now;
    Alas, thou wilt get cold.
Beatrice.   Alas, the fear keeps that out;   95
    My heart will find no quiet till I hear
    How Diaphanta, my poor woman, fares.
    It is her chamber, sir, her lodging chamber.
Vermandero. How should the fire come there?
Beatrice. As good a soul as ever lady countenanced,   100
    But in her chamber negligent and heavy;

---

93. *Dog at*] skilled in dealing with.
singed] i.e. burned from bravely getting so close to the fire.
100. *countenanced*] favoured, gave her patronage.
101. *heavy*] sluggish (or perhaps implying that she was a heavy sleeper).

She 'scaped a mine twice.
Vermandero.   Twice?
Beatrice.   Strangely twice, sir.
Vermandero. Those sleepy sluts are dangerous in a house,
    An they be ne'er so good.

Enter DE FLORES.

De Flores.   O poor virginity!
    Thou hast paid dearly for't.
Vermandero.   Bless us! What's that?   105
De Flores. A thing you all knew once—Diaphanta's burnt.
Beatrice. My woman, oh, my woman!
De Flores.   Now the flames
    Are greedy of her; burnt, burnt, burnt to death, sir!
Beatrice. O my presaging soul!
Alsemero.   Not a tear more,
    I charge you, by the last embrace I gave you   110
    In bed before this raised us.
Beatrice.   Now you tie me;
    Were it my sister, now she gets no more.

Enter Servant.

Vermandero. How now?
Servant. All danger's past, you may now take your rests, my
    lords; the fire is throughly quenched. Ah, poor gentle-   115
    woman, how soon was she stifled!
Beatrice. De Flores, what is left of her inter,
    And we as mourners all will follow her.

---

102. *She . . . twice*] Diaphanta twice narrowly escaped an accident of some kind. (An emendation to 'ruin' has been suggested.) Beatrice's 'twice' may allude to the fact that Diaphanta successfully passed the virginity test, and was not detected by Alsemero when she took Beatrice's place.

104. *An . . . good*] no matter how good they may be as servants.

104. S.D.] Some editors emend the stage direction so that De Flores enters with the body of Diaphanta. But there is nothing in the rest of the scene to make this definite, and lines 54–5 above weigh against it.

111. *tie*] constrain.

112. *she . . . more*] I will weep no more tears for her.

115. *throughly*] thoroughly.

I will entreat that honour to my servant,
Ev'n of my lord himself.
Alsemero.   Command it, sweetness.   120
Beatrice. Which of you spied the fire first?
De Flores.   'Twas I, madam.
Beatrice. And took such pains in't too? A double goodness!
    'Twere well he were rewarded.
Vermandero.   He shall be.
    De Flores, call upon me.
Alsemero.   And upon me, sir.
                              Exeunt. [*Manet* DE FLORES.]
De Flores. Rewarded? Precious, here's a trick beyond me!   125
    I see in all bouts, both of sport and wit,
    Always a woman strives for the last hit.   *Exit.*

[v. ii]

Enter TOMAZO.

Tomazo. I cannot taste the benefits of life
    With the same relish I was wont to do.
    Man I grow weary of, and hold his fellowship
    A treacherous bloody friendship; and because
    I am ignorant in whom my wrath should settle,   5
    I must think all men villains, and the next
    I meet (whoe'er he be) the murderer
    Of my most worthy brother.—Ha! What's he?

Enter DE FLORES, *passes over the stage.*

    Oh, the fellow that some call honest De Flores;
    But methinks honesty was hard bested   10
    To come there for a lodging—as if a queen
    Should make her palace of a pest-house.
    I find a contrariety in nature

---

120. *my lord*] Alsemero.
125. *Precious*] i.e. by God's precious body (an oath).
here's . . . me] this is a better piece of trickery than I could have thought of.
126. *sport*] (1) game such as fencing; (2) sexual play.
wit] wit-combat.

V.ii.10. *hard bested*] hard pressed, in desperate need.
12. *pest-house*] hospital for plague victims.

Betwixt that face and me; the least occasion
Would give me game upon him. Yet he's so foul,   15
One would scarce touch him with a sword he loved
And made account of; so most deadly venomous,
He would go near to poison any weapon
That should draw blood on him. One must resolve
Never to use that sword again in fight,   20
In way of honest manhood, that strikes him;
Some river must devour't; 'twere not fit
That any man should find it.—What, again?

Enter DE FLORES.

He walks o' purpose by, sure, to choke me up,
To infect my blood.
De Flores.   My worthy noble lord!   25
Tomazo. Dost offer to come near and breathe upon me?
                                        [*He strikes him.*]
De Flores. A blow!   [*He draws his sword.*]
Tomazo.   Yea, are you so prepared?
    I'll rather like a soldier die by th'sword
    Than like a politician by thy poison.   [*He draws.*]
De Flores. Hold, my lord, as you are honourable.   30
Tomazo. All slaves that kill by poison are still cowards.
De Flores. [*Aside*] I cannot strike; I see his brother's wounds
    Fresh bleeding in his eye, as in a crystal.
    [*To Tomazo*] I will not question this. I know you're
        noble;
    I take my injury with thanks given, sir,   35
    Like a wise lawyer, and as a favour

14–15. *the least . . . him*] I would take any opportunity to attack him.

16. *a sword he loved*] a sword that the owner regarded as precious.

17. *so*] De Flores is so.

29. *politician*] Machiavellian plotter, more likely to use poison than fight
an honourable duel.

33. *Fresh bleeding*] Perhaps alluding to the belief that a murdered man's
wounds began to bleed again if the murderer came near the corpse.

as . . . crystal] as though seen through glass; as in a crystal ball.

34. *question this*] make you account for your action.

36. *Like . . . lawyer*] perhaps implying that a lawyer will tolerate a humiliating blow so that he can claim damages for himself.

36–7. *and as . . . gave it*] I will regard the blow as a token of friendship
given by an honourable man.

Will wear it for the worthy hand that gave it.
[*Aside*] Why this from him, that yesterday appeared
So strangely loving to me?
Oh, but instinct is of a subtler strain;   40
Guilt must not walk so near his lodge again.
He came near me now.   *Exit.*
Tomazo. All league with mankind I renounce for ever,
Till I find this murderer; not so much
As common courtesy but I'll lock up.   45
For in the state of ignorance I live in,
A brother may salute his brother's murderer,
And wish good speed to th' villain in a greeting.

Enter VERMANDERO, ALIBIUS, *and* ISABELLA.

Vermandero. Noble Piracquo!
Tomazo.   Pray keep on your way, sir;
I've nothing to say to you.
Vermandero.   Comforts bless you, sir.   50
Tomazo. I have forsworn compliment, in troth I have, sir.
As you are merely man, I have not left
A good wish for you, nor for any here.
Vermandero. Unless you be so far in love with grief
You will not part from't upon any terms,   55
We bring that news will make a welcome for us.
Tomazo. What news can that be?
Vermandero.   Throw no scornful smile
Upon the zeal I bring you; 'tis worth more, sir.
Two of the chiefest men I kept about me
I hide not from the law, or your just vengeance.   60

41.] A guilty person must avoid the place where his crime was committed.
42. *came near me*] almost found me out.
43. *league*] alliance, friendship.
44–5. *not . . . up*] I will not even use the everyday courtesies of greeting.
51. *compliment*] polite courtesies.
52. *As . . . man*] since you are a man, and since I have renounced mankind.
55. *You*] that you.
56. *will*] that will.
60.] Vermandero offers Tomazo a choice: he can either hand Antonio and Franciscus, apparently his brother's murderers, over to the law to undergo trial and punishment, or take private vengeance on them himself.

Tomazo. Ha!

Vermandero. To give your peace more ample satisfaction,
 Thank these discoverers.

Tomazo.   If you bring that calm,
 Name but the manner I shall ask forgiveness in
 For that contemptuous smile upon you.   65
 I'll perfect it with reverence that belongs
 Unto a sacred altar.   [*He kneels.*]

Vermandero.   Good sir, rise. [*He raises him.*]
 Why, now you overdo as much o' this hand
 As you fell short o' t'other.—Speak, Alibius.

Alibius. 'Twas my wife's fortune (as she is most lucky 70
 At a discovery) to find out lately
 Within our hospital of fools and madmen
 Two counterfeits slipped into these disguises;
 Their names, Franciscus and Antonio.

Vermandero. Both mine, sir, and I ask no favour for 'em. 75

Alibius. Now that which draws suspicion to their habits,
 The time of their disguisings agrees justly
 With the day of the murder.

Tomazo.   Oh, blest revelation!

Vermandero. Nay more, nay more, sir—I'll not spare mine
  own
 In way of justice—they both feigned a journey 80
 To Briamata, and so wrought out their leaves;
 My love was so abused in't.

Tomazo.   Time's too precious
 To run in waste now; you have brought a peace
 The riches of five kingdoms could not purchase.
 Be my most happy conduct; I thirst for 'em. 85

---

63. *these discoverers*] i.e. Alibius and Isabella.

64–5.] You yourself shall specify the way in which I shall atone for my contemptuous behaviour just now.

66. *perfect*] complete, bring to perfection.

73. *these disguises*] Alibius may be holding the clothing worn by Antonio and Franciscus.

75. *mine*] my servants.

76. *habits*] disguise costumes.

80. *both*] apparently an oversight; according to IV.ii.7–8 one of them pretended to be going to Valencia.

81. *wrought . . . leaves*] obtained permission to be absent.

82. *My love*] my trust in them.

85. *conduct*] guide.

> Like subtle lightning will I wind about 'em,
> And melt their marrow in 'em.   *Exeunt.*

[v. iii]

Enter ALSEMERO *and* JASPERINO.

Jasperino. Your confidence, I'm sure, is now of proof.
    The prospect from the garden has showed
    Enough for deep suspicion.
Alsemero.   The black mask
    That so continually was worn upon't
    Condemns the face for ugly ere't be seen—   5
    Her despite to him, and so seeming-bottomless.
Jasperino. Touch it home then. 'Tis not a shallow probe
    Can search this ulcer soundly; I fear you'll find it
    Full of corruption. 'Tis fit I leave you.
    She meets you opportunely from that walk;   10
    She took the back door at his parting with her.

                          Exit JASPERINO.

Alsemero. Did my fate wait for this unhappy stroke
    At my first sight of woman?—She's here.

Enter BEATRICE-JOANNA.

Beatrice. Alsemero!
Alsemero.   How do you?
Beatrice.   How do I?

86–7.] Lightning was supposed to melt marrow in the bones but not disfigure the skin. Tomazo's vengeance will be subtle and devastating.

V.iii.1. *of proof*] confirmed (used of armour which has been tested).

3. *The black mask*] This might seem to allude to De Flores' ugliness, but the context suggests that lines 3–6 apply to Beatrice. The 'black mask' may be her hypocrisy, or perhaps she literally wore a black mask to protect her complexion (compare Shakespeare's *Romeo and Juliet*, I.i.227–8, and *Measure for Measure*, II.iv.79).

7. *Touch it home*] make a searching investigation.

10–11.] It looks as though Alsemero and Jasperino have entered the castle after watching a meeting of Beatrice and De Flores in the castle garden (line 2 above). Alsemero now waits for Beatrice to enter the castle and catch up with him.

13. *my . . . woman*] Beatrice is the first woman he has loved (but also hinting at Adam's experience).

Alas! How do you? You look not well.   15
Alsemero. You read me well enough. I am not well.
Beatrice. Not well, sir? Is't in my power to better you?
Alsemero. Yes.
Beatrice.   Nay, then you're cured again.
Alsemero. Pray resolve me one question, lady.
Beatrice.   If I can.
Alsemero. None can so sure. Are you honest?   20
Beatrice. Ha, ha, ha! That's a broad question, my lord.
Alsemero. But that's not a modest answer, my lady.
    Do you laugh? My doubts are strong upon me.
Beatrice. 'Tis innocence that smiles, and no rough brow
    Can take away the dimple in her cheek.   25
    Say I should strain a tear to fill the vault,
    Which would you give the better faith to?
Alsemero. 'Twere but hypocrisy of a sadder colour,
    But the same stuff. Neither your smiles nor tears
    Shall move or flatter me from my belief: 30
    You are a whore!
Beatrice.   What a horrid sound it hath!
    It blasts a beauty to deformity;
    Upon what face soever that breath falls,
    It strikes it ugly. Oh, you have ruined
    What you can ne'er repair again.   35
Alsemero. I'll all demolish, and seek out truth within you,
    If there be any left. Let your sweet tongue
    Prevent your heart's rifling; there I'll ransack
    And tear out my suspicion.
Beatrice.   You may, sir;

---

18. *Nay . . . cured*] I will do anything to make you well, so consider yourself cured.

19. *resolve*] answer.

20. *honest*] chaste, honourable.

24. *rough brow*] angry frown.

25. *her*] Innocence's, personified in the previous line.

26. *strain . . . vault*] force out a fit of weeping to fill up the sky with tears.

28. *sadder*] darker, graver.

29. *stuff*] cloth, material.

37–8. *Let . . . rifling*] Speak the truth so that I do not need to tear open
your heart.

'Tis an easy passage. Yet, if you please,   40
Show me the ground whereon you lost your love.
My spotless virtue may but tread on that,
Before I perish.
Alsemero.   Unanswerable!
A ground you cannot stand on; you fall down
Beneath all grace and goodness, when you set   45
Your ticklish heel on't. There was a visor
O'er that cunning face, and that became you;
Now impudence in triumph rides upon't.
How comes this tender reconcilement else
'Twixt you and your despite, your rancorous loathing,   50
De Flores? He that your eye was sore at sight of,
He's now become your arm's supporter, your
Lip's saint!
Beatrice.   Is there the cause?
Alsemero.   Worse: your lust's devil,
Your adultery!
Beatrice.   Would any but yourself say that,
'Twould turn him to a villain.
Alsemero.   'Twas witnessed   55
By the counsel of your bosom, Diaphanta.
Beatrice. Is your witness dead, then?
Alsemero.   'Tis to be feared
It was the wages of her knowledge; poor soul,
She lived not long after the discovery.
Beatrice. Then hear a story of not much less horror   60
Than this your false suspicion is beguiled with.

---

41. *ground*] (1) basis, cause; (2) area on which to walk or stand.
your love] your love for me.
43. *Unanswerable!*] The evidence against you is so overwhelming that you
cannot challenge it.
46. *ticklish*] (1) unsettled, fickle; (2) easily excited sexually.
visor] mask, disguise.
47. *became you*] made you attractive.
50. *your despite*] someone despised by you.
52–3. *your / Lip's saint*] the one you worship (with prayers and kisses).
53. *cause*] accusation.
54. *adultery*] partner in adultery.
56. *counsel . . . bosom*] confidential adviser.

To your bed's scandal, I stand up innocence,
Which even the guilt of one black other deed
Will stand for proof of: your love has made me
A cruel murd'ress.
Alsemero.   Ha!
Beatrice.   A bloody one;   65
I have kissed poison for't, stroked a serpent.
That thing of hate, worthy in my esteem
Of no better employment, and him most worthy
To be so employed, I caused to murder
That innocent Piracquo, having no   70
Better means than that worst to assure
Yourself to me.
Alsemero.   Oh, the place itself e'er since
Has crying been for vengeance, the temple
Where blood and beauty first unlawfully
Fired their devotion and quenched the right one.   75
'Twas in my fears at first; 'twill have it now.
Oh, thou art all deformed!
Beatrice.   Forget not, sir,
It for your sake was done; shall greater dangers
Make the less welcome?
Alsemero.   Oh, thou shouldst have gone
A thousand leagues about to have avoided   80
This dangerous bridge of blood; here we are lost.
Beatrice. Remember I am true unto your bed.
Alsemero. The bed itself's a charnel, the sheets shrouds

62.] i.e. In answer to your bed's scandal I stand up (set up, put forward)
innocence.

64. *your love*] my love for you.

72–6.] Compare I.i.1–12.

74–5.] where sexual desire and physical beauty became objects of worship
instead of true religion.

76. *'twill . . . now*] (1) now my fears are confirmed; (2) the place is determined to have vengeance now.

79–81. *thou . . . blood*] i.e. you should have made a detour of a thousand
leagues rather than cross over to your goal by means of murder. (A league is
approximately three miles.)

83. *charnel*] charnel-house, place for storing the bones of the dead.

For murdered carcasses. It must ask pause
What I must do in this. Meantime you shall   85
Be my prisoner only; enter my closet.

      Exit BEATRICE-JOANNA.

I'll be your keeper yet. Oh, in what part
Of this sad story shall I first begin?—Ha!

     Enter DE FLORES.

This same fellow has put me in.—De Flores!
De Flores. Noble Alsemero?
Alsemero.   I can tell you   90
 News, sir; my wife has her commended to you.
De Flores. That's news indeed, my lord; I think she would
 Commend me to the gallows if she could,
 She ever loved me so well. I thank her.
Alsemero. What's this blood upon your band, De Flores?   95
De Flores. Blood? No, sure, 'twas washed since.
Alsemero.   Since when, man?
De Flores. Since t'other day I got a knock
 In a sword and dagger school; I think 'tis out.
Alsemero. Yes, 'tis almost out, but 'tis perceived, though.
 I had forgot my message; this it is: 100
 What price goes murder?
De Flores.   How, sir?
Alsemero.   I ask you, sir;
 My wife's behindhand with you, she tells me,
 For a brave bloody blow you gave for her sake
 Upon Piracquo.
De Flores.   Upon? 'Twas quite through him, sure.
 Has she confessed it?
Alsemero.   As sure as death to both of you,   105

---

86. *prisoner*] Alsemero locks and unlocks his closet (see IV.i.17–18) as
Beatrice and De Flores enter separately and come out together at line 143.

89. *put me in*] shown me where to start.

91. *her . . . you*] sent you her greetings, asked to be remembered.

95. *band*] cuff or collar.

98. *out*] washed out, removed.

102. *behindhand*] still owing payment.

104. *Upon*] This might imply that De Flores merely struck Alonzo a
superficial blow, when in fact he gave him a mortal wound.

And much more than that.

De Flores.   It could not be much more;
   'Twas but one thing, and that—she's a whore.

Alsemero. It could not choose but follow. O cunning devils!
   How should blind men know you from fair-faced saints?

Beatrice. (Within) He lies, the villain does belie me!   110

De Flores. Let me go to her, sir.

Alsemero.   Nay, you shall to her.—
   Peace, crying crocodile, your sounds are heard!—
   Take your prey to you; get you in to her, sir.

                              Exit DE FLORES.

   I'll be your pander now; rehearse again
   Your scene of lust, that you may be perfect   115
   When you shall come to act it to the black audience
   Where howls and gnashings shall be music to you.
   Clip your adult'ress freely; 'tis the pilot
   Will guide you to the Mare Mortuum,
   Where you shall sink to fathoms bottomless.   120

         Enter VERMANDERO, ALIBIUS, ISABELLA, TOMAZO,
                  FRANCISCUS, *and* ANTONIO.

Vermandero. Oh, Alsemero, I have a wonder for you.

Alsemero. No, sir, 'tis I, I have a wonder for you.

Vermandero. I have suspicion near as proof itself
   For Piracquo's murder.

Alsemero.   Sir, I have proof
   Beyond suspicion for Piracquo's murder.   125

Vermandero. Beseech you hear me; these two have been
      disguised
   E'er since the deed was done.

Alsemero.   I have two other
   That were more close disguised than your two could be,

---

109. *blind*] blinded by passion.

112.] Crocodiles were supposed to shed hypocritical tears while seizing their prey (here De Flores).

115. *perfect*] able to perform your role perfectly.

116. *black audience*] devils in hell.

118. *Clip*] embrace.

119. *the Mare Mortuum*] the Dead Sea, here signifying hell.

126. *two*] Presumably Vermandero points directly at Antonio and Franciscus.

128. *close*] closely, impenetrably.

E'er since the deed was done.

Vermandero. You'll hear me!—these mine own servants—   130

Alsemero. Hear me—those nearer than your servants,
That shall acquit them, and prove them guiltless.

Franciscus. That may be done with easy truth, sir.

Tomazo. How is my cause bandied through your delays!
'Tis urgent in blood, and calls for haste.   135
Give me a brother alive or dead:
Alive, a wife with him; if dead, for both
A recompense, for murder and adultery.

Beatrice. (*Within*) Oh, oh, oh!

Alsemero.   Hark, 'tis coming to you.

De Flores. (*Within*) Nay, I'll along for company.

Beatrice. (*Within*)   Oh, oh!   140

Vermandero. What horrid sounds are these?

Alsemero. Come forth, you twins of mischief!

Enter DE FLORES *bringing in* BEATRICE-JOANNA [*wounded*].

De Flores. Here we are. If you have any more
To say to us, speak quickly; I shall not
Give you the hearing else. I am so stout yet,   145
And so, I think, that broken rib of mankind.

Vermandero. An host of enemies entered my citadel
Could not amaze like this. Joanna! Beatrice! Joanna!

Beatrice. Oh, come not near me, sir; I shall defile you.
I am that of your blood was taken from you   150
For your better health; look no more upon't,

---

130. *You'll hear me!*] Will you listen to me?

134. *bandied*] tossed about.

138. *adultery*] Tomazo cannot yet know of Beatrice's adultery with De Flores; presumably he regards her as Alonzo's 'wife' (see line 137), and considers her marriage to Alsemero to be a kind of adultery.

139. *Hark . . . you*] i.e. Tomazo's recompense is coming.

145. *stout*] valiant; resolute; strong.

146. *rib of mankind*] Beatrice; an obvious allusion to Genesis, 2.21–3.

147. *entered*] who have entered.

150. *that . . . was*] that infected part of your blood which was. The metaphor is of medical blood-letting, and Vermandero is imagined as holding the container of bad blood which has been purged from him, uncertain what to do with it. Beatrice tells him not to debate the problem any more, but to throw the blood to the earth, whence it will run into the common sewer.

But cast it to the ground regardlessly.
Let the common sewer take it from distinction.
Beneath the stars, upon yon meteor
Ever hung my fate, 'mongst things corruptible;   155
I ne'er could pluck it from him. My loathing
Was prophet to the rest, but ne'er believed;
Mine honour fell with him, and now my life.
Alsemero, I am a stranger to your bed;
Your bed was cozened on the nuptial night,   160
For which your false bride died.

Alsemero.   Diaphanta!

De Flores. Yes, and the while I coupled with your mate
    At barley-break; now we are left in hell.

Vermandero. We are all there; it circumscribes here.

De Flores. I loved this woman in spite of her heart;   165
    Her love I earned out of Piracquo's murder.

Tomazo. Ha! My brother's murderer!

De Flores.   Yes, and her honour's prize
    Was my reward. I thank life for nothing
    But that pleasure; it was so sweet to me
    That I have drunk up all, left none behind   170
    For any man to pledge me.

Vermandero.   Horrid villain!
    Keep life in him for further tortures.

De Flores.   No!
    I can prevent you; here's my penknife still.
    It is but one thread more [*Stabbing himself*]—and now 'tis
        cut.

---

153. *distinction*] the condition of being distinct or separate.

154–5.] A deliberate contrast is intended between 'stars' and 'meteor' (i.e. De Flores). In Elizabethan cosmology the stars were pure, fixed, and eternal; meteors belonged to the sublunary world of change and decay, and were transitory, of evil omen, and the result, or indication, or corruption.

156–7. *My loathing . . . believed*] My hatred of De Flores was prophetic of what would happen, but I ignored the warning.

159.] Alsemero and Beatrice have not yet made love.

163. *barley-break*] See note on III.iii.167.

167. *her honour's prize*] (1) the taking of her virginity; (2) the destruction of her reputation.

171. *pledge*] offer a toast to.

Make haste, Joanna, by that token to thee: 175
Canst not forget, so lately put in mind,
I would not go to leave thee far behind.   *Dies.*
Beatrice. Forgive me, Alsemero, all forgive;
'Tis time to die, when 'tis a shame to live.   *Dies.*
Vermandero. Oh, my name is entered now in that record   180
Where till this fatal hour 'twas never read.
Alsemero. Let it be blotted out, let your heart lose it,
And it can never look you in the face,
Nor tell a tale behind the back of life
To your dishonour. Justice hath so right   185
The guilty hit, that innocence is quit
By proclamation, and may joy again.
Sir, you are sensible of what truth hath done;
'Tis the best comfort that your grief can find.
Tomazo. Sir, I am satisfied; my injuries   190
Lie dead before me. I can exact no more,
Unless my soul were loose, and could o'ertake
Those black fugitives that are fled from thence,
To take a second vengeance; but there are wraths
Deeper than mine, 'tis to be feared, about 'em.   195
Alsemero. What an opacous body had that moon
That last changed on us! Here's beauty changed
To ugly whoredom; here, servant obedience
To a master sin, imperious murder;

175–7.] The exact syntax of these lines is hard to determine. The 'token'
seems to be the wound De Flores has just given himself, which will remind
Beatrice that he is unwilling to be parted from her even in death.

180. *record*] the heavenly record of human deeds and misdeeds.

182–5. *Let . . . dishonour*] Let this dreadful event be deleted from the
record (see previous note); forget about it, and it will never confront you,
or give rise to slander behind your back.

185–7. *Justice . . . proclamation*] Justice has so rightly struck down the
guilty that the innocent have been cleared of suspicion by public proclamation of the truth.

188. *sensible*] aware.

190. *my injuries*] those who injured me.

193. *Those black fugitives*] the damned souls of Beatrice and De Flores.

194–5. *but . . . 'em*] but it is to be feared that hellish wrath, more terrible
than mine, is consuming and punishing them.

196. *opacous*] opaque, obscured (a sinister omen).

197. *That . . . us*] during its most recent twenty-eight-day cycle.

I, a supposed husband, changed embraces   200
  With wantonness, but that was paid before.
  Your change is come too, from an ignorant wrath
  To knowing friendship. Are there any more on's?
Antonio. Yes, sir; I was changed too, from a little ass as I was
  to a great fool as I am, and had like to ha' been changed   205
  to the gallows, but that you know my innocence always
  excuses me.
Franciscus. I was changed from a little wit to be stark mad,
  Almost for the same purpose.
Isabella. [*To Alibius*]   Your change is still behind,
  But deserve best your transformation.   210
  You are a jealous coxcomb, keep schools of folly,
  And teach your scholars how to break your own head.
Alibius. I see all apparent, wife, and will change now
  Into a better husband, and never keep
  Scholars that shall be wiser than myself.   215
Alsemero. [*To Vermandero*] Sir, you have yet a son's duty
      living;
  Please you, accept it. Let that your sorrow,
  As it goes from your eye, go from your heart.
  Man and his sorrow at the grave must part.

EPILOGUE

Alsemero. All we can do to comfort one another,   220
  To stay a brother's sorrow for a brother,

---

201. *wantonness*] i.e. Diaphanta.
  before] earlier, by her death.
202. *Your*] Tomazo's.
203. *on's*] of us.
206. *innocence*] (1) guiltlessness; (2) idiocy.
209. *Your . . . behind*] Alibius's change, from a foolish jealous husband to
a wise one, is yet to come.
210.] Show that you deserve to be changed.
212. *break . . . head*] make you a cuckold.
216.] Alsemero offers the duty as a son to Vermandero which had been
lacking in Beatrice as a daughter.
217. *that your sorrow*] that sorrow of yours.
218. *As . . . eye*] i.e. as you weep tears.
220. *All we*] all that we.
221. *stay*] bring to an end.

To dry a child from the kind father's eyes,
Is to no purpose; it rather multiplies.
Your only smiles have power to cause re-live
The dead again, or in their rooms to give   225
Brother a new brother, father a child;
If these appear, all griefs are reconciled.

Exeunt omnes.

FINIS.

222.] to dry the eyes of a kind father weeping for his daughter.
224. *Your only smiles*] only your smiles (those of the audience).